7 Nonprofit Income Streams

Open the Floodgates to Sustainability!

Karen Eber Davis

7 Nonprofit Income Streams: Open the Floodgates to Sustainability!

One of the **In the Trenches**™ series

Published by
CharityChannel Press, an imprint of CharityChannel LLC
30021 Tomas, Suite 300
Rancho Santa Margarita, CA 92688-2128 USA

CharityChannel.com

ISBN Print Book: 978-1-938077-65-4 | ISBN eBook: 978-1-938077-66-1

Library of Congress Control Number: 2014948809

13 12 11 10 9 8 7 6 5 4 3 2 1

Printed in the United States of America

This and most CharityChannel Press books are available at special quantity discounts for bulk purchases for sales promotions, premiums, fundraising, or educational use. For information, contact CharityChannel Press, 424 Church Street, Suite 2000, Nashville, TN 37219 USA. +1 949-589-5938.

Publisher's Acknowledgments

This book was produced by a team dedicated to excellence; please send your feedback to editors@charitychannel.com.

We first wish to acknowledge the tens of thousands of peers who call CharityChannel.com their online professional home. Your enthusiastic support for the **In the Trenches**™ series is the wind in our sails.

Members of the team who produced this book include:

Editors

Acquisitions Editor: Linda Lysakowski

Art Editor: Kim O'Reilly

Comprehensive Editor: Bill Smith

Copy Editors: Michele Komen Nelson and Jill McLain

Production

In the Trenches Series Design: Deborah Perdue

Layout Editor: Stephen Nill

Administrative

CharityChannel LLC: Stephen Nill, CEO

Marketing and Public Relations: Linda Lysakowski and John Millen

About the Author

Karen Eber Davis is a leading authority on income growth strategies for nonprofits. She helps leaders generate the ideas, resources, and money they need to fulfill their goals and create extraordinary impact.

For over twenty years, Karen has advised nonprofit organizations such as The Salvation Army, Habitat for Humanity, The American Red Cross, Ringling College of Art and Design, Meals on Wheels PLUS, and many others.

Karen is a contributing author to *YOU and Your Nonprofit Board: Advice and Practical Tips from the Field's Top Practitioners, Researchers, and Provocateurs* (CharityChannel Press, 2013). She has published over two hundred articles in a variety of publications, including *Advancing Philanthropy*, CharityChannel Press at CharityChannel.com, *Nonprofit World*, and *The Nonprofit Times*. Her monthly newsletter, *Added Value*, and column, "The Ingenious Nonprofit," inspire leaders to find ways to realize more funding and more supporters to accomplish their mission.

Karen graduated *magna cum laude* from the University of Connecticut and earned her MBA in finance from the University of South Florida.

Dedication

To Connor, my best friend. Thank you for encouraging me, word by word. You are amazing!

Author's Acknowledgments

The nonprofit community is full of remarkable people who do heroic work. I'm so grateful to the many executive directors and CEOs who responded to my invitation to share their experiences and successes raising income. Without you, this book would not be so meaty and inspirational. Your wonderful stories surpassed my already-high expectations. I also want to thank my current and former clients who inspired me to create this tool so that you, too, can have adequate resources to accomplish your nonprofit's important work. Many of these stories wove their way into this text.

Thank you to the staff at the United Way Nonprofit Connection in Houston for your help connecting me with outstanding nonprofits in the Houston Community. Pam Williams with Nonprofit Finance Pros, Inc., thank you for connecting me with Susan Motley, the executive director of the Medical Society of Virginia Foundation. Thank you, Linda Mansperger, with The Hermitage Artist Retreat, for your help connecting me with the Florida Association of Museums and, through them, with Jennifer Beam with Bok Tower Gardens. Mary Helen Kress, I appreciate your connecting me to Pam Nabors, president and CEO of Workforce Central Florida. And thank you, Pam Nabors, for connecting me with several other workforce boards.

Even more gratitude goes out to two peers who encouraged me in this endeavor. Laura Mikuska, with the Mikuska Group, endured the play-by-play in our regular meetings. Jen Filla, with Aspire Research Group, helped with graphics and was my first in-the-field reader. If you can snag either or both of these women to partner with you on a project, your nonprofit will be galaxies better for it. Finally, thanks to the folks at CharityChannel Press who said yes. Line by line, you help me become a better writer. Day by day, your work strengthens nonprofits.

Contents

Foreword

I first met Karen several years ago when we coproduced, audio-designed, and with several other consultants led an international teleclass series called "Serving on Nonprofit Boards Is Good Business." I was instantly struck with Karen's incredible wealth of knowledge about the plethora of income sources for nonprofits and her gift of communicating the complex—and sometimes mysterious—aspects of nonprofit income.

The number-one question I'm asked as a professional fundraising auctioneer and consultant is "How can I make more money at my fundraising auction or charity event?" Sadly, far too many nonprofits rely heavily on special-event fundraising as a key source of income. Bouncing from event to event is a surefire recipe for board burnout, staff stress, and the demise of your donor base—it's inherently shortsighted and unsustainable.

My top predictor of success is how well the nonprofit organization integrates all aspects of a special event into the overall advancement plan. Now more than ever, as nonprofits struggle for greater income and resources to support their mission, they must create successful, sustainable income—and that means having a strategy and a plan.

Insightful, indispensable, and inspiring, Karen has written the essential book that every nonprofit leader, volunteer, and board member should read, share, and keep on the corner of the desk. Her book helps you clarify, organize, and understand your options.

You need a strategy and a plan. Karen's book helps you by exploring the seven income sources and by sharing dozens of success stories and real-life examples. I love her informative and provocative sidebars, which are chock-full of practical tips, real-life examples, stories from the real world, to-do lists, and even helpful cautionary insights.

It is clear from reading Karen's book why she is in high demand as a fundraising consultant. It is obvious that she not only really "knows her stuff" but also guides nonprofits and boards to implement comprehensive, creative, and imminently doable income plans.

Karen demystifies how to use the seven funding streams to discover what really works and how build a customized income plan. She clearly and compellingly shares how nonprofits can get the results they want and need.

Benjamin Franklin said, "An investment in knowledge pays the best interest." I invite you to read Karen's book, act on her strategies, and invest in your nonprofit.

Clearly passionate about nonprofit fundraising and income generation, Karen makes the seven income sources and strategies easily understood as well as fascinating, thought provoking, and inspiringly accessible.

Kathy Kingston, CAI, BAS
Professional auctioneer and consultant
President, Kingston Auction Company

Introduction

I've worked with nonprofit organizations for over twenty years. So far, every organization—and there have been thousands—was eager for more income. For some, more income meant expanding their great work. Others wanted more money to keep up with inflation and provide competitive wages. For too many, the situation was dire or about to become dire. Threats were on the horizon. They faced the need to close essential programs. They even faced threats to their existence.

Are nonprofit income challenges a must? Must nonprofits always be in a crisis because of income? Must obtaining funds always be difficult, time consuming, and stressful? The answer is a resounding no! Might there be a different way? Yes! Many nonprofits succeed in creating viable and sustainable income streams.

For example:

- ◆ Goodwill sells your donated goods while providing jobs, job training, and other services. For Goodwill, individual donations and retail sales provide stable income.

- ◆ Habitat for Humanity affiliates solve their income challenge with three key sources: resale stores, homeowner mortgage payments, and donations.

- ◆ Tampa's Museum of Science and Industry (MOSI) charges admission. It also obtains income from its gift store, summer camp, IMAX Dome, sponsorships, and individual donations.

- ◆ Some of New York City's Metropolitan Museum of Art's income results from admission and/or membership fees. However, only

26 percent of the $200 million budget comes from these two sources. It earns much more from individual donations.

◆ CommunityHealth in Chicago provides $10 million per year in health care to the uninsured. More than three-quarters of its budget comes from donated services, inventory, and labor. Individual donations provide fewer than one in five dollars. Even less funding comes from the government.

Your nonprofit can also generate sustainable income. How can you do this? Develop a dependable income strategy and an income plan, and then follow both to obtain it. What do you need to know to create this strategy? First, understand the different income sources available to your nonprofit.

Part One of this book looks at nonprofit income challenges and provides a glimpse of the seven income streams that you can use to create sustainable income for your nonprofit. The heart of the book explores each of the seven nonprofit income streams in-depth. These seven sources and all their variations are where you can obtain the income you need. I devote a chapter to each source and examine Chapter Two, "Stream Two— Individual Giving" in three sections because of its complexity. Briefly, the seven sources are:

1. Mission Income

This is earned income you receive from a customer who pays the nonprofit to receive a mission-related service or product (for example, the income from ticket sales for your theater production). Mission income can range from a token fee to one that covers costs and provides resources for others who cannot afford a fee, or support for general operations.

2. Individual Giving

Gifts from individuals, which can range from pennies to fortunes, are the largest source of donated income. Individuals can provide many benefits other than cash. For example, when individuals partner with your nonprofit, they can give their ideas, share their problem-solving skills, and make introductions to other community leaders.

3. Government Funding

Income from governments includes grants, contracts, earmarks, and public-private partnerships. Some nonprofits are government mandated and funded with public resources. Others, while not birthed by government decree, earn significant income from government entities. Most nonprofits, with some exceptions such as religious bodies that seek funds to proselytize, can identify one or more potential government-funding sources.

4. Foundations and Other Grantmaking Entities

Approximately 125,000 foundations exist in the United States and Canada. To meet their goals, foundations provide grants to nonprofits, usually via a competition. Foundations range in size from small family organizations where relatives meet yearly to disburse funds to international organizations with large staffs. Each is unique. Each has its own parameters and goals for distributing money. Your nonprofit organization's ability to access this income depends on the fit of your mission and proposal with the foundation's goals. This category also includes other nonprofit organizations that provide grants, such as United Ways, Rotary Clubs, and Junior Leagues.

5. Businesses Supporting Nonprofits

Corporations also provide income to nonprofits. Who can take advantage of these opportunities? Most commonly, nonprofits that reach customers with whom for-profits would like to communicate. With some creativity, most nonprofits can tap business funding. To grow this source, nonprofits should examine the needs of businesses around them, find places where customers overlap, and design ways to partner with a business to reach mutual goals. While all nonprofit income sources have an element of quid pro quo, this exchange is more overt with business sources.

6. Unrelated Income Opportunities

Over time, nonprofits have created heaps of earned-income opportunities that provided them income without any mission benefits, except that these profits help the nonprofit. Examples include room rentals and beverage sales. Nonprofits often use unrelated income to pay for necessary but unattractive items, such as cleaning supplies and employment taxes. While unrelated income may require different tax treatments (check with your accountant), unrelated income's flexibility—you can spend it on whatever is needed—guarantees its continued appeal.

7. In-Kind Donations: When Cash Isn't King

The last income stream available to nonprofits is not cash. Instead, it is gifts of services or goods that make cash unnecessary. In-kind gifts include the meeting room that a local church provides you once per month for board meetings. It includes donated clothes and food. It consists of the fee waiver the city provides your annual festival. It comprises all volunteers, such as those used by a college to help with orientation. Almost all nonprofits obtain some type of in-kind gifts. It is important to include these gifts as you plan your income, because you can often obtain in-kind donations that free up cash for other necessities.

Part Two of this book provides information to help you use the seven funding streams. This section helps you gather information by studying what others are doing in your field—especially organizations that are successful at obtaining income. Learning what works in the real world will help you fine-tune your ideas and test your assumptions.

With this information, you're ready to build a customized income strategy and a plan to create sustainable income. To help, I provide best-practice suggestions on how to develop a strategy and a plan and how to evaluate new opportunities coming over the transom.

Most of all, my goal is to give you hope. Your nonprofit can, like thousands of others, obtain the income you need. Which of the seven sources or combination of sources can help you achieve sustainable income? The chapters ahead will help you find out.

As you read, you will encounter different sidebars. Here is a rundown on their content:

- ◆ **Definition:** The meaning of a word or term used in this book or by those in the nonprofit field.

- ◆ **Example:** A concrete instance illustrating the meaning of a concept.

- ◆ **Food for Thought:** An idea to ponder and consider.

- ◆ **Important!** Something significant to remember as you strategize and plan.

◆ **Observation:** An idea of particular note gleaned from writing this book and/or from work in the field.

◆ **Practical Tip:** A helpful tip to use today.

◆ **Principle:** A fundamental tenet or tenets about nonprofit income.

◆ **Stories from the Real World:** A real-world example of a way a nonprofit obtains income.

◆ **To-Do Lists:** Tasks to put words into action.

◆ **Quote:** Advice from someone in the field who said "it" very well.

◆ **Watch Out!** Be careful. This is something to avoid.

Getting the Most Out of this Book

◆ Read the book for understanding. As you read, consider why people provide income to your nonprofit. Which income streams do you already tap? Which income streams can you add or refine? Consider what language you use when you talk about income opportunities. What would it mean if you looked at your opportunities through the eyes of whoever provides the money?

◆ If you don't already have one at your nonprofit, develop a strategy for long-term income sustainability. You will find guidelines in Chapters Eight and Nine. In the long term, regular shortfalls are no fun and unnecessary. Identify and combine the income streams to use as a base and discern those that provide supplementary resources.

◆ Finally, no matter where you are in developing sustainable income at your nonprofit, read to find ideas that successful nonprofits now use. You can adapt them or use them as springboards for new ideas. Start with the Story from the Real World sidebars before skimming for others. Don't forget to consider concepts from other fields. You can often profitably transform them. Build on the successes of these nonprofits and find at least three ideas to use. Check out additional stories and updates on my website, kedconsult.com.

Part One

An Introduction to Sustainable Income

Why does a sector that calls itself nonprofit spend so much time worrying about obtaining adequate income to do its work? One reason is that nonprofit income is confusing. Some people know about only a few of the opportunities available. Not only that, but some popular myths about nonprofit income are incorrect, as well. This first part of the book introduces you to the challenges of nonprofit income and the seven available nonprofit income streams, and it explains how understanding both challenges and streams will help you earn more income.

To help you understand nonprofit income, I've sorted the streams of income based on who provides it, who organized it, and the size of each group's contributions. By doing this you can see that three groups provide the vast majority of income. They are customers who purchase mission services or mission products, individuals who donate, and governments.

Three additional groups provide income, but a lot less of it. They are foundations and other grant-giving entities, corporations, and unrelated income opportunities—that is, people who purchase goods and services without mission content. In-kind gifts from all of the above sources comprise the final stream of income. While not cash, in-kind income is valuable.

To prepare your nonprofit to obtain more income, Chapters One through Seven examine in depth the seven nonprofit income streams and each of their characteristics, benefits, and challenges.

How to Find Funding for Your Nonprofit

The following topics are covered in this section:

◆ The nonprofit income challenge

◆ What's usually blamed?

◆ The four causes of the income challenge

◆ The seven nonprofit income streams: an introduction

◆ Your opportunity: sustainable income

◆ Examples of success

The Nonprofit Income Challenge

The board of a nonprofit that served two hundred children with disabilities was content. Things were going well. Despite seven years of government cuts, the board had managed, with effort, to maintain a balanced budget that allowed the nonprofit to provide an array of services. Or so the board thought. One month after it hired a new financial expert, she informed the board that instead of breaking even, the nonprofit was deep in the red. For years, staff had created and presented balanced budgets—based solely on bequests. Fortunately for its beloved donors, but unfortunately for the nonprofit, the projected deaths had not occurred.

The number-one battle nonprofit leaders face is funding. Without funding, nonprofits cannot achieve their mission. Lack of income is the main reason nonprofits fail. In a *Nonprofit World* survey, nonprofit leaders overwhelmingly rated "increasing fundraising revenue" as their top need. When *GuideStar* surveyed leaders, it asked, "What is the **greatest** challenge your organization faces?" Forty-six percent of the respondents selected the option "Finding the money to accomplish our mission," which far surpassed the other options. "I can fill a hundred workshops a year *if* they have the word 'fundraising' in their title," states Margaret Linnane with Rollins College, Philanthropy & Nonprofit Leadership Center.

Even if your nonprofit doesn't list finding money as its top challenge, money probably is on your wish list. Every nonprofit seeks new income opportunities. With more money you can fulfill your mission. Money and the resources money can buy create the mission results that justify a nonprofit's existence.

For example, what would your board do with an extra $100,000? What would happen if I promised to give your organization $100,000 if you could develop five intelligent ways to invest it in an hour? I guarantee that within forty minutes, you would identify a dozen viable ideas and be plotting how to increase my gift to $250,000. It is no surprise that Linnane can fill workshops on funding. It is not astonishing that nonprofit leaders identify income development as their key challenge. Nonprofit funding is a huge need in a competitive market. It is life and mission for the work nonprofit leaders want to do.

> ### Fundraising Magic
>
> *I can fill a hundred workshops a year if they have the word 'fundraising' in their title.*
>
> —Margaret Linnane, executive director, Rollins College, Philanthropy & Nonprofit Leadership Center.
>
> **" "**

Can your nonprofit obtain sustainable income? The answer is a definite yes! By understanding how to use and combine the seven different nonprofit funding sources discussed in this book, leaders like you can find income solutions. By studying the sources, leaders can discover ways to enhance existing streams and new opportunities.

What's Usually Blamed? Frequently Used Excuses for Nonprofit Income Challenges

To begin our work to improve your nonprofit funding, here is a look at some of the excuses used for inadequate nonprofit income:

Lack of Commitment

Nonprofit leaders and people who support them are passionate. They tackle numerous, even unpleasant, activities to support their missions. After a meeting, Anna rushed to ask me, "I'm on the board of the ballet. Do you have any great ideas for galas?" Nonprofits abound with commitment and passion. Lack of commitment does not create nonprofit income challenge.

Lack of Ideas

Although people like Anna fear they lack ideas, an idea shortage is not the cause. Nonprofits usually have the equivalent of a messy garage full of income ideas. One goal of this book is to help you organize your possibilities and find those that will bring you income success. Lack of ideas is not the source of the nonprofit funding challenge.

It's the Economy

When the tide goes out, you see what is invisible at high tide. Likewise, recent global financial struggles revealed previously unseen weak nonprofit income solutions. Even though more nonprofits fail during economic downturns, the nonprofit income challenge is not new. In a 2009 study, based on data from before the recent Great Recession, the Urban Institute found that 68 percent of human service nonprofits reported problems with government payments not covering the full cost of contracted services. This and other shortages existed before—and will continue long after—any economic downturn. The economy is not the source of the nonprofit funding challenge.

> ### Fundraising Magic
>
> *The image of the mighty bank and the inept nonprofit no longer apply.*
>
> —Andrea Perraud, guest writer, Young Nonprofit Professionals Network of New York City Blog
>
>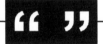

Nonprofits Are Inept

Some people think that individuals select nonprofit careers because they "can't make it" elsewhere. Income challenges, therefore, reflect ineptness. In reality, nonprofit missions are difficult to fund. Governments can rely on taxing authority. Businesses sell goods and services to benefit consumers. Only nonprofits, which lack authority to tax and often sell intangible goods, rely heavily on voluntary income support. The nonprofit world is filled with educated, well-trained professionals. Ineptness is not the cause of the challenge.

It's Just Part of Being a New Nonprofit

While income challenges often are more apparent in new organizations, they also occur in mature ones. Some nonprofits never find adequate ways to make ends meet. For others, former solutions provide dwindling resources, e.g., collecting dimes no longer works for the March of Dimes. Over time, all nonprofit income strategies require tweaking. At other times, even well-honed solutions must be abandoned. The nonprofit funding challenge is not solely for new organizations.

While every nonprofit would like more income, some nonprofits solve their income challenges and develop diverse, stable funding. You do not need to experience ongoing nonprofit income challenges. Since other nonprofits find nonprofit income solutions, you can too. More than fifty examples are scattered throughout this book. The nonprofit income challenge is not a foregone conclusion.

The Four Causes of the Income Challenge

If lack of commitment, lack of ideas, the economy, ineptness, and newness are not at the heart of the nonprofit funding challenge, what is? Let's examine the four principal causes.

1. Nonprofit Income Is Confusing

At an annual meeting, halfway through a discussion about revenue, a long-time leader raised a hand and asked, "Since we are a nonprofit, are we allowed to make a profit?" The short answer is yes, nonprofits can make a profit. Not only can they make a profit to survive, they must. However, if your leadership faces uncertainties or fundamental questions about obtaining income, you have a roadblock the size of ten trucks in your path. Why so large? Instead of moving forward with certainty to obtain income, you must constantly circle back to educate the unsure.

2. Lack of Knowledge

How do nonprofits earn income? How does your nonprofit earn it? How much income do you need? What is possible? What is likely? In workshops, when I ask leaders to draw their organization's income pie chart, most can't sketch one. To make decisions, leaders must understand the origins of income. What is more, leaders need to understand which sources of funding are most likely to provide a nonprofit the most income with the least long-term effort. To reach your income goals, you need knowledge.

In addition to lack of knowledge, unorganized ideas and possibilities create fog. Board members, staff, volunteers, and even consultants contribute to the fog by offering income ideas and platitudes. Fog collects around the seven nonprofit income sources and subcategories. Left unsorted and unprioritized, this fog blocks the way like rush hour traffic blocks intersections.

3. Lack of a Viable Strategy and Plan

Too many nonprofits lack a viable strategy and plan to get them from inadequate to adequate income. In an ideal world, the US Internal Revenue Service, the Canada Revenue Agency, and other countries' governmental agencies would refuse to issue permission for any organization to become a nonprofit without a viable strategy.

Too many nonprofits leave the starting box with a flimsy strategy patched together en route. Few have a strategy powering a beeline to success. Some survive for years like an old car rattling and belching down the road. Others create strategies and plans based on wishful thinking. Some are based on anticipated expenses.

A new development director shared her nonprofit's projected budget. The director's job was to obtain $250,000 in foundation grants, $250,000 in corporate funding, and $50,000 in individual giving in the remaining ten months of the year. Yet the nonprofit made only about $50,000 from all of these sources the previous year. What's the origin of these income projections? "I'm pretty sure they were made up," the development director grimaced.

A viable strategy and a plan to match will work, if you

Can the Nonprofit Profit?

Yes, a nonprofit organization may earn a profit. The difference is that the profit must stay within the organization and not go to stockholders. Over time, you must either earn a profit or at least cover 100 percent of all costs of mission activities, overhead, and future capacity.

 practical tip

build them on opportunities, logic, past history, market conditions, your culture, and your skills. This book helps you examine your opportunities, explore viable strategies, and plan to help your nonprofit create sustainable income. How can I make that promise? You, like every other nonprofit, have only seven sources.

4. Limited Solutions

As Joe Nonprofit Leader struggled to fall asleep, he counted money sheep. Some sheep gathered and jumped calmly over the fence. "Yes," he yawned, "the money sheep from tuition." He snuggled with his spouse. "Ah, the supply donation sheep. And look, the small flock of lambs we earn from renting the building occasionally." The other money sheep refused to jump. Joe startled, fully awake. "Dang," he thought, throwing off the sheet, "what if those individual gifts don't come in?"

Joe's sleeping challenges illustrate a math problem that sits predominantly in the brains of nonprofit leaders. The problem focuses on two kinds of income: the easy and the difficult, or the "givens" and the "gap." The givens include all income and in-kind gifts that a nonprofit organization consistently earns year to year. The gap is all the money that must be raised

to balance the budget—anxiety-causing uncertainty. When the gap is large, it causes widespread fear—or, in Joe's case, disturbed sleep. To fill the gap, many nonprofits tweak current income efforts year to year and hope for the best. The nonprofit Joe leads, for example, is a child care center. It serves sixty preschool students, and it must obtain $500,000 per year to remain open.

The Givens (the Easy Part)

Each of the center's sixty students pays $611 per month for twelve months, or $7,332 per year. Although the center maintains a waiting list, vacancies still occur when student enrollment begins and ends. In total, tuition income equals about $430,000. The center also receives $30,000 of in-kind resources, mainly school supplies, from volunteer and business donors.

The Gap (the Hard Part)

The biggest headache for the center and most nonprofits is securing this "everything else." This is the gap. Each year, the center sponsors a special event that nets $20,000, seeks foundation grants that net around $10,000, and receives individual donations of at least $10,000. At least that's the plan. Most years, everyone worries until these gifts arrive. Even though mission income represents around 86 percent of the budget, like many other nonprofits, most of the energy is spent closing the gap. The options that leaders usually think will grow income instead just tweak existing revenue streams.

The Child Care Center's Givens and Gap Income Equations

The Equation—Before

Program cost, overhead, and future capacity:	$500,000
The Givens	
Less in-kind resources	$30,000
Cash needed	$470,000
Customer fees (mission income)	$430,000
The Gap ($40,000)	
Individuals: Special event and holiday gifts	$30,000
Foundation grant(s)	$10,000
Balance (desired)	$0

Facing the Challenge

Using the income solutions in this book, the center revised its income strategy and plans. It increased in-kind resources by $5,000. It unbundled its services to earn another $7,500 by charging fees for early and late drop-offs. It beefed up individual giving to bring in another $5,000. The center then identified three potential corporate sponsors for a special event. The rest of the income solution remains the same. The changes re-energized the leaders. The proposed gap was smaller than ever, and if all went well, there will be money at year's end for a rainy-day fund.

The Equation—After

Program cost, overhead, and future capacity:	$500,000
The Givens	
Less in-kind resources	$35,000
Cash needed	$465,000
Customer fees (mission income)	$437,500
The Gap ($27,500)	
Individuals: Special event and holiday gifts	$24,000
Foundation grant(s)	$7,500
Corporate sponsorships	$6,000
Balance (for reserves)	$10,000

With this plan in place, leaders could invest more time increasing the center's program quality and streamlining student transition into the center. The next year, if finances remain strong, they will return to discuss creating a satellite site and a program to engage grandparents and seniors to provide more resources and potential new donors.

By examining the infrastructure of nonprofit funding, the information in this book helps you clear the fog and increase your knowledge. You will be encouraged to develop a viable strategy based on a realistic assessment of your options. Finally, it will invite you to broaden your options so that you examine all your opportunities and find solutions that allow you to focus on your mission.

By using the tools and information in this book, you can identify your income opportunities and create strategies and plans to obtain sustainable income. Be forewarned that even with solid plans and awareness, you face challenging work. No one can remove that. However, by using the information here, you can learn how to create long-term stable income. Your nonprofit funding challenge becomes an opportunity for renewal and growth, not something to keep you awake at night.

The Seven Nonprofit Income Sources: An Introduction

Sources of nonprofit income can be organized into seven streams based on who provides the income to your nonprofit.

No-Sweat Pop Quiz

Of the seven sources of nonprofit income, which one provides the most money?

a) In-kind donations

b) Mission income (income from providing mission activities)

c) Individual donations

d) Governments

e) Corporations

f) Foundations and grants

g) Unrelated income (money from non-mission activities)

The answer is b. Mission income provides the greatest amount of nonprofit income. Does this surprise you? If so, consider for a minute the funding of nonprofit hospitals, colleges, housing facilities for people with special needs, and Habitat for Humanity home sales. Beyond large-ticket items, keep in mind theater ticket sales, private school after-school fees, and membership dues.

If you didn't score 100 percent on this quiz, you are not alone. Perhaps you selected individual gifts. They *are* extremely important. If so, you probably remembered famous philanthropists like Bill Gates, Warren Buffet, and George Soros. Or perhaps you are aware of the collective power of donors who give small amounts? Individuals provide the largest source of *donated* income, but they are not the *largest* source of all nonprofit income.

Government income is also a popular choice. If you selected this, it is likely that you are familiar with recipients of large government contracts or grants. Government funding, along with mission income and individual donations, are the three biggest sources of nonprofit income.

A surprisingly large segment of people, both inside and outside the nonprofit world, selected foundations and other grant-giving organizations. If you

---

Sector-wide Nonprofit Income

The pie chart illustrates six of the seven sources of all nonprofit funding. You probably already noticed that it doesn't show in-kind donations, which will be discussed later.

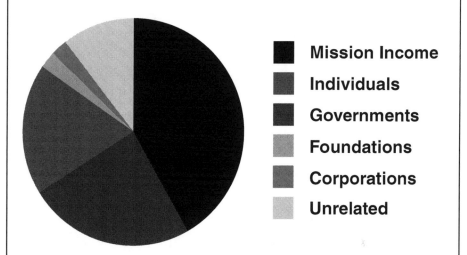

■ **Mission Income**

■ **Individuals**

■ **Governments**

■ **Foundations**

■ **Corporations**

■ **Unrelated**

Pie Chart Notes

◆ The pie chart is based on estimates and data from the Nonprofit Quarterly, Giving USA, and The Aspen Institute.

◆ The relative amounts the funding sources provide stay basically the same year to year.

◆ This does not represent an ideal-income pie chart. It represents the results of nonprofit searches for funding as a whole. Your nonprofit's pie chart can look very different and still be highly successful.

food for thought

selected this option, is it because you watch or listen to public broadcast stations that frequently thank foundation sponsors? Or have you heard that grants are available—somewhere? Do you believe that if you can find the right people, your nonprofit will obtain them as donors? While knowledge is very important when it comes to grants, unfortunately, grants are only a small portion of all nonprofit income.

Glancing at the pie chart in the *Food for Thought* sidebar on the previous page, you may decide that nonprofits have minimal income options. In fact, nonprofits have more than most entities. For funding, governments rely almost entirely on taxes. Businesses sell services and products. The multiple options available to nonprofits have helped bring about the sector's success. But these options also can result in confusion about which methods to use to solve the income challenge. Within these seven major categories, numerous options and possibilities exist, including your nonprofit-income solution.

Invite Your Leadership for Dessert

Do you want to help your leaders gain new insight about your organization's income? Invite them to tackle this exercise over dessert.

Goal: To learn about current income sources and to explore opportunities.

Time: Allow one hour, as part of a retreat or a meeting.

Steps:

1. Hand each participant a paper with a six-inch circle drawn on it.

2. List your income categories on a board.

3. Ask each participant to draw a pie chart for your organization based on a best guess of your current income sources.

4. Share the results, and discuss the ranges and guesses.

5. Post your existing-income pie chart.

6. Share one or more of the following pie charts:

     ◆ The compilation for all nonprofits income sources found in Chapter One

◆ If you are part of a national group, a compilation chart from that group

◆ A chart from your industry segment, e.g., animal welfare, congregations, or employment specialists

7. Ask for surprises, insights, and learning points. Share what you learned putting the exercise together.

8. Suggested discussion questions:

◆ What is our ideal pie chart?

◆ Do we invest our training, resources, and leadership for each source in proportion to earnings?

◆ Does this make sense?

◆ Are we missing any funding streams?

◆ If we want to enlarge or change the proportions of our pie, what actions must we take?

◆ What steps will we take next?

9. After you plan, serve dessert—pie, of course.

Preparation:

◆ Do a dry run of the exercise. Modify as needed.

◆ Gather supplies: pencils, markers, newsprint or a whiteboard to take notes, and circle handouts. Create pie charts.

◆ Collect dessert supplies: pies, plates, forks, napkins, and utensils.

With your understanding of how nonprofits earn income as a whole, this section briefly examines the different income streams. With these seven streams, you can create healthy, stable nonprofit organizations. Later chapters focus on each source in depth. As you read, note which sources you already tap and any additional sources that appeal to you.

Income Stream 1: Customer Buyers (i.e., Mission Income)

Mission income is funding you receive from a customer who pays to receive a mission-related service or product. It is, for example, the income from ticket sales for your theater production. Mission income can range from a token fee that covers some costs to a fee that covers overhead—or one that supports those who cannot afford a fee.

Income Stream 2: Dedicated Individuals (i.e., Individual Giving)

If you guessed that individual giving is the largest source of income, you would not be alone. Seventy-five percent or more of all *donated* money (versus *all* money) given to nonprofit organizations originates with individuals. Within this funding source, many techniques exist to earn donations, such as annual appeals, major gifts, special events, and planned gifts, including bequests (gifts people leave to nonprofits through their wills).

Income Stream 3: Governments (i.e., Government Funding)

Income from governments includes grants (a competitive process), contracts (possibly competitive), earmarks (inserted into a government's budget by a supportive elected official), and public/nonprofit partnerships. The many levels of government and quasi-government agencies that provide funding to nonprofits may include city, state, provincial, and national governments.

Income Stream 4: Foundations and Other Grantmaking Entities

Approximately 125,000 foundations exist in the United States and Canada. This category also includes other nonprofit entities that provide grants, such as local Rotary Clubs. To meet their goals, foundations provide grants to individual nonprofit organizations, usually via a competitive process. Foundations range in size from small family foundations where family members meet once yearly to decide on disbursements to nationwide foundations with multiple full-time staff. The latter often have an international focus and provide millions in funding. Each is unique. Each has its own parameters and goals to distribute money.

Income Stream 5: Businesses Supporting Nonprofits

Big-picture corporate and business contributions are a small piece of the nonprofit funding pie. However, when talking about a percentage or two of a $1.5 trillion nonprofit sector, this income stream may be worth considering for your nonprofit. Corporate income varies from a local bank buying a table at your special event to a retailer offering a percentage of sales on purchases to a corporation becoming a major sponsor. Corporate funding usually takes the form of grants, cause marketing, and sponsorships.

Income Stream 6: Unrelated Income Opportunities

What do the following have in common?

◆ Tampa Bay Watch rents out its community room with water views of Tierra Verde Bay.

◆ The Women's Resource Center runs a resale shop.

◆ The Hippodrome State Theatre sells wine and snacks to patrons during intermission.

◆ Your lobby has a soda machine.

Answer: They all provide nonprofits with income unrelated to its mission. Unrelated income is similar to a for-profit's income that is distant from its core business, e.g., a grocery store selling toys.

Income Stream 7: In-Kind Donations

The last income source is not cash. Instead, it is gifts of services or physical items that make cash unnecessary. The yearly value of in-kind donations to nonprofits is in the billions, if not trillions, of dollars. While much appreciated, such income is often unrecorded and inconsistently measured. Some nonprofits, like The Food Bank of Houston and CommunityHealth in Chicago, base their services largely on in-kind support. Almost all nonprofits obtain in-kind gifts, like pet food at animal shelters, paper and supplies for schools, or the volunteer labor given by your finance committee. Included in this category is all discounts given to nonprofits because of their nonprofit status.

The funding your nonprofit needs will come from some combination of these seven sources. As you read the list, you will recognize streams your nonprofit taps and perhaps others where you have an interest. Most nonprofits focus on three or four sources for the majority of funding. Ideally, the sources you choose will fit your mission, culture, and skills. You'll also want sources that offer the most income with the greatest efficiency.

To Recap

◆ You can earn the income you need from these seven nonprofit funding streams: mission-related income, dedicated individuals, governments, foundations, corporations, unrelated income, and in-kind donations. Other nonprofits solve their income challenges using these sources, and you can too!

◆ Long before the Great Recession, funding challenges plagued nonprofit organizations. In part, it's the nature of the sector. This chapter started with the true story of a nonprofit whose staff balanced its budgets with hoped-for bequests. With some staff changes, that organization survived and went on to explore earned-income opportunities as a way to stabilize and grow.

◆ The good news is that their nonprofit funding challenge, and yours, is solvable. The bad news is that, left unsolved, this challenge can easily become a life-and-death struggle for your organization.

Chapter One

Stream One—Mission Income

IN THIS CHAPTER

···→ About mission income and its possibilities

···→ Will it work for you?

···→ Benefits and challenges

···→ Examples of success

For nonprofits as a whole, mission income is the largest single source of revenue. Yet mission income is one of the least discussed nonprofit income streams. This chapter explores mission income. First, we look at its components by studying some examples. Then I briefly discuss how to identify opportunities. To help you decide if this income stream is worthy of more study at your nonprofit, I share major benefits and challenges. As you read, consider the possibilities for your nonprofit.

Boley Centers provides safe, affordable housing. To fulfill its mission, it rents 1,200 housing units for people with special needs. In return, the occupants pay Boley rent. This creates *mission income* for Boley Centers, its main income source.

Fees for service, ticket sales, and rents, as earned by the Boley Centers, qualify as mission income. Even if money is your main objective, the mission you also achieve with this income stream offers a strong logical and emotional reason to pursue it. The mission accomplished while earning the income is what differentiates this funding stream from the similar sounding "Unrelated Income," discussed in Chapter Six.

Bok Tower Gardens, located in Lake Wales, Florida, earns mission income from ticket sales. In the 1970s, it acquired Pinewood Estate, a 12,000-square-foot 1920s-era mansion that adjoins its property. Originally, the mansion hosted board meetings and special events. During the day, visitors took docent-led tours for an additional six-dollar fee, paid in its visitor center.

Imagine the expenses associated with maintaining a 12,000-square-foot 1929 mansion. For years, Bok Tower Gardens leaders discussed what to do about the mansion, as it consistently lost money. Then the leaders designed *and* implemented a four-pronged solution:

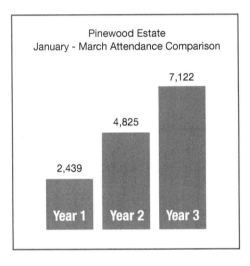

◆ Guests are offered the choice of a general admission adult ticket that includes the gardens or, for six dollars more, a combo ticket that includes entrance to Pinewood Estate.

◆ Instead of tours at specific times, Pinewood Estate is open for self-guided tours for four hours daily.

◆ Docents inside the mansion help visitors enjoy it.

◆ Staff added new signage around and in the mansion that cost less than $2,000.

The results, as illustrated, included a 300 percent increase in attendance *and* income.

Bok Tower Gardens is one of my favorite mission-income examples. It demonstrates that by paying attention and experimenting with what you already are doing, you can increase your income and achieve more mission.

In the past, many nonprofits, and perhaps even you, ignored the mission-income stream. Many assume they already are maximizing it. If this is you, consider not only Bok Tower's experience but also the one at MacDonald Training Center, a nonprofit serving developmentally delayed adults. When a new staff member was hired, she began reviewing the agency's contracts. She discovered a mission-income contract that had not been renegotiated in seven years. The center quickly renegotiated the contract and earned more income.

Why Do People Give Mission-Income Money to Nonprofits?

Customers purchase mission services or goods because it offers clear value. They want a product or service because it adds to their lives. Some customers actually prefer nonprofit providers—a vote for your good work and a benefit of being a nonprofit.

The Structure of Mission Income

To better understand the structure of mission income, let's examine Bright Beginnings, a nonprofit new to this source. Bright Beginnings provides many services to families and children to help the latter achieve their potential, including academic tutoring. Organization income is primarily government funded. To reduce dependence on government money, leadership decided to use agency skills to seek mission income.

At a charter school in a new service area, Bright Beginnings launched a fee-based tutoring program. The tutoring helps children prepare for Florida's standardized test, the FCAT (Florida Comprehensive Assessment Test). Helping children master this test meets Bright Beginnings' mission to help children reach their potential. The charter school endorses Bright Beginnings' tutoring because of the agency's staff expertise and the stellar results Bright Beginnings achieves elsewhere. Parents invest in tutoring because their children need help, and they understand its value.

What do you need to earn mission income at your nonprofit? You need three things: a mission, a product or service, and a fee (funding). Each component is essential. For some nonprofits, mission income serves a supporting role, providing smaller, but still useful, revenue. Bright Beginnings' fee-based tutoring sits in the mission-income sweet spot, the place where all three circles interlock in the "Anatomy of Mission Income" illustration:

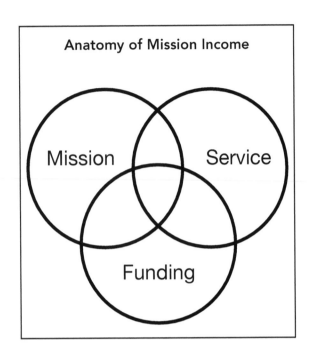

Anatomy of Mission Income

Mission   Service

Funding

◆ Mission: Helping children reach their full potential.

◆ Service: Tutoring.

◆ Funding: The fees parents pay.

Is your idea to increase funds a mission-income idea? It is if it contains all three components.

Finding Mission-Income Opportunities

Mission-income ideas are everywhere. To create a list of possibilities, write all the ideas under discussion at your nonprofit. The ideas might work by themselves. Or they may inspire a new idea. For most nonprofits, thinking about who needs or might benefit from their mission generates multiple possibilities. For Bok Tower, the knowledge that they were losing money on a fascinating house stirred staff to act.

Use the examples throughout this book for inspiration and ideas. Also, answer these three questions to identify multiple mission-income opportunities:

◆ What new service can you offer for your current clients?
Example: Add after-hours care.

◆ Which new customers can you serve with existing services?
Example: Open a new office in an adjacent city.

◆ How can you serve new markets and new clients for a fee?
Example: Offer environmental tourism at your remote, but
beautiful, site.

In my work, I find most nonprofits have, with a little prompting, plenty of
ideas. The challenge comes with selecting from among them to identify

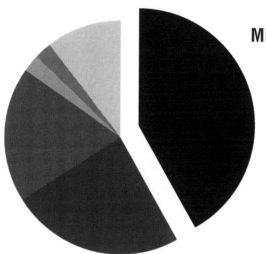

Mission Income

The Big Three

Mission income, individual donations, and government funds represent
the big-three players in nonprofit income streams. Collectively, they
provide 85 percent of a nonprofit's cash income. Mission income is
earned revenue. It represents a "great bargain" because you earn money
and accomplish your mission. Social entrepreneurship is a special kind of
mission income that often involves a separate legal entity. It is beyond
the scope of this book.

principle

those most practical, lucrative, and beneficial. To find them, you will probably have to experiment with a number of options.

How Much?

An important consideration for nonprofit leaders exploring mission income is its income potential. How much money can you earn? The range is broad. Some groups, such as hospices, hospitals, and residential centers, earn the vast majority of their income. Other nonprofits pride themselves on never earning a dime. Most nonprofits delight at earning modest amounts, as they positively impact the mission.

A solid goal for most nonprofits getting started is to earn between 5 and 10 percent of annual income from mission income in a year or two. It often helps to try several activities and quickly eliminate those that fail to create strong interest and solid cash flows. The more you try, the more you will learn and the sooner you will see your earned income grow. To obtain a better estimate for endeavors

---

Three-year Development Cycle

Entrepreneurs often begin their business ventures with this three-year cycle in mind:

◆ Year 1: Starve.

◆ Year 2: Break even.

◆ Year 3: Succeed.

◆ Anticipate a similar development cycle for your major mission-income ventures.

observation

---

that require upfront investments, interview other leaders with similar, successful ventures. Chapter Eight discusses this in depth.

What if no similar venture exists? If we discuss this over coffee, I will argue this point and help you brainstorm. With 1.5 million nonprofits and nearly 28 million businesses in the United States alone, someone has done something similar. Still stuck? Find a creative thinker to help you identify similar opportunities.

In any case, you will want to evaluate your mission-income opportunities in terms of overall organizational strategy. For instance, mission opportunities that allow you to reach critical groups of new customers can be especially worthwhile. Many might earn you less than 100 percent of their costs but still represent huge successes. Of course, how much you earn is based, in part, on how much you charge. You have a variety of choices, which we'll look at shortly.

The Benefits of Mission Income

Each nonprofit income source fits nonprofits differently. Does the work associated with mission income suit your nonprofit's personality, culture, and values?

To decide if mission income is "for you," compare and contrast its benefits with the benefits of other income streams. Here are five benefits of mission income:

1. Independence

Nonprofits exert a great deal of control over mission income. In contrast, an individual donor can change plans and give money to a long-lost niece pursuing a medical degree. The government can cancel your contract. Your main corporate sponsor can abandon a strategy that once made you an ideal partner. With mission income, you determine the price, do the marketing, serve the customers, and earn the income. Since you understand your mission best, your nonprofit is in the ideal position to identify services that create mission income at a price you can sustain.

2. Closeness to Customers

Mission income creates close contact between you and the customers to whom you provide value. In the past, you might have thought it was tough finding a good landlord to serve your customers. However, when you become a landlord as part of earning mission income, you perceive landlord-hood differently and can, therefore, create better experiences for your customers. Proximity allows you to fulfill needs and, ideally, earn even more mission. Mission-income activities provide a close feedback loop between you and your customers.

3. Sustainability

Mission income sustainability is so consistent that many nonprofits assume this income will remain essentially the same year to year. While rarely as exciting as receiving a huge donation, mission income's reliability is very reassuring. Additionally, many social service nonprofits worry about creating unnecessary dependency in those they serve. Charging for services reduces this risk. Fees can also eliminate stigmas associated with receiving charity. Most nonprofits serve people who can afford to pay at least a token fee. Many Salvation Army homeless shelters charge for housing after several free nights.

4. Efficiency

Since mission income provides both income and mission, it is very efficient. The other nonprofit income streams require personnel to convert income into services.

5. Higher Value

If you have ever run a free event, you know that many people who make reservations do not attend. Putting a price on your services increases their value in consumers' eyes. In all likelihood, if you charge for your services they will be more valued by those you serve. Fees add a positive tension between the nonprofit and its consumers: Value is expected in return for payment.

Warren Cox with SPCA Florida found that the public started valuing dogs more when the SPCA increased its fees to adopt them. By charging more, the SPCA increased income, encouraged better treatment of the animals, and demonstrated to new owners that owning pets involves expenses.

The Challenges of Mission Income

Several challenges confront nonprofits as they seek mission income:

Conflicts over Beliefs

Wendy stood before the local government grant-review panel and answered its question about fees. "Our services are free," she began. "When my son was little, I had enough on my hands getting him to services without having to worry about paying for them. We believe parents who have a child with disabilities have enough challenges without adding the burden of fees too." Values may exist in your organization that make simply looking at mission income seem wrong.

Values may exist that make mission income seem less attractive than donated income. Are some nonprofit income streams superior to others? Perhaps. If you believe that donated funds are superior to earned funds, this value might lead to lukewarm mission-income efforts and results. On the other hand, if the staff of Bok Tower Gardens decided that funds to support Pinewood Estate had to come from individual donations, hundreds of their guests would be missing the opportunity to explore the Great Gatsby-like mansion.

Values about fees often run deep. While cultural shifts, discussed next, involve a lot of "we have never done it that way before," values ask questions about what it means to pursue your mission. If asking some customers to pay for services negatively affects your ability to fulfill your mission, then you might need to avoid it.

And if you believe, as Wendy does, that your customers are already burdened and also must not have to pay regardless of their ability or that mission income is an "also ran" choice, you will need to do some intense strategic thinking to determine how your nonprofit will be funded and what role, if any, mission income will play.

If you have these kinds of concerns, schedule board time to discuss your organization's values regarding fees. Answer questions, such as:

◆ What role might mission income play in our income strategy?

◆ When and where are fees appropriate?

◆ What positive benefits can be realized by charging a fee?

Need for Cultural Changes

If your organization has never charged for services, adding a mission-income stream will require a cultural shift, or a different frame of reference for the work. For instance, a group that supported cancer patients told me it could never charge patients for services. It was against the group's charter. Period. Not yet content to let it rest, I asked, "Who else, besides your primary customers, receives value from your

services?" With encouragement, they began exploring the possibility of providing services to medical groups and hospitals by offering feedback

---

Missing Income?

The Senior Friendship Center provides a health clinic for seniors. To cover overhead, it added a sliding-scale fee. The clinic, however, generated little revenue. Puzzled, staff investigated. They learned that some volunteer doctors were advising patients to tell the assistant at checkout that they could not afford to pay, even if they could.

In response, the nonprofit developed training sessions for the clinic's volunteers and staff, wherein they shared the center's budget challenges and details about uncovered expenses, including soap, water, and utility bills. Attendees learned that the clinic would close without the wonderful volunteers *and* the fees. Over time, leadership communicated why the fees were essential and began to change the culture. Fees became a normal part of doing business.

stories from the real world

---

on the medical services offered. This was extremely valuable mission-enhancing information. With it, people experiencing cancer could, by giving feedback to the medical community, improve client experiences and help future patients. Members of the medical community might learn what is most important to patients and how to serve and attract them. Because of the relationships the nonprofit had with both parties, it was in a unique position to provide this value for a fee. For this organization, even considering fees represented a major rethinking of what the organization was and how it might operate. It would be a cultural shift. You also may live in a culture that dictates "you shall not charge fees."

Don't underestimate the size of this task. Making a cultural shift is no small matter. It takes time, energy, and focus. To support the shift, recognize that pursuing mission income will require new behaviors and skills. Staff and volunteers will find using these behaviors and skills uncomfortable. It will help if they understand the why behind them.

Viability

Finding an idea and creating a fee-based program that creates mission and produces solid funding can be a challenge. In the United States, just 96 percent of new businesses survive two years. Litter from failures fill our lives, including audiocassette tapes and kitchen gadgets that require odious cleaning. Many of the entities that created these items went on to develop new products. Your nonprofit also might need to work through several ideas until you identify viable candidates for your skills, setting, and market.

Evaluating Your Work

By entering a more overtly competitive market space, a nonprofit's work will often require more critical evaluation. Not everyone is ready to grapple with this. You might be badly ranked by Yelp! It takes a healthy self-esteem and a true desire to "be all you can be," to listen, and to improve. You can charge for your services and accept the feedback as a gift. Make your services worthy and believe in them.

Southeastern Guide Dogs is a great example. It decided to be the top seeing-eye-dog school in the nation. By preferring quality over quantity, it created a viable nonprofit that competes primarily with other guide-dog schools. It offers the community several mission-income opportunities.

> ### Sure Thing?
>
> "What surprises me most is how some services that look like sure things don't work," says Susan Motley, executive director of the Medical Society of Virginia Foundation. "For example, providing continuing education for people who are required by law to have it seems like a natural fit for an association. Yet it can be hard to monetize. When you study the true cost of such programs, you might just break even. On the other hand, some activities like our quality improvement for physicians have been very successful. One needs to experiment and invest."
>
> **observation**

Skills

Nonprofits involved in mission income must continually grow skills to conceive of and manage opportunities. For many nonprofits, obtaining mission income requires adding new expertise:

◆ Identify potential opportunities.

◆ Test the market to determine if an opportunity is viable.

◆ Determine price.

◆ Market products or services.

◆ Comply with IRS or Canada Revenue Agency rules.

◆ Collect fees.

◆ Refine services and products midstream.

◆ Evaluate if the effort is worth pursuing long term.

Donor Confusion

Many people support the Girl Scouts by purchasing their cookies. This mission-income opportunity teaches girls entrepreneurism, marketing, and similar skills. The funds earned from cookie sales are not the only income needed. Yet cookie sales confuse some would-be Girl Scout donors. They believe that by buying cookies, they have done their part to support this worthwhile nonprofit. Your mission income efforts can send a similar unintended message to potential donors. If you engage in mission income and seek individual donations, you will need to be vigilant about keeping donors and potential donors informed about unmet needs that their donations support.

How Much to Charge—An Opportunities Continuum

To expand your thinking, the chart on the next page illustrates a set of choices about what you might charge customers. On the left side of the chart, we start with sliding-scale fees. As we move toward the right, you earn more of the money it takes to offer a product. Charges to the left of the vertical line represent fee options where your customers do not pay for the full cost of the service but contribute to it. Naturally, when customers do not pay for all of the costs of a program, you should identify other income streams to cover these expenses, e.g., a corporate donation.

To the right of the vertical line, customers pay the full cost of the service and make donations. Here people begin to be individual donors *and* customers. You use the surplus for other agency needs or to invest in future products.

Consider the following fees with both your mission and unrelated income opportunities:

◆ *Sliding scale.* A fee charged based on the customer's income. Often used in government-funded programs. For instance, if your family income is below a certain amount, you pay one dollar. Families with more income pay ten dollars.

◆ *Direct cost.* A fee based on the out-of-pocket expenses a nonprofit spends to provide the service. No fees are collected for administration, building use, overhead, or the like. You run a summer sports camp, and the fees charged cover the cost of running it when you add it to other existing programs.

◆ *Overhead costs.* A fee based on all the costs of running the program and of running a viable nonprofit. Your campers pay a fee that covers direct expenses plus a proportion of other costs incurred by the organization, like the executive director's salary and audit. Large nonprofits, like universities, often have a preestablished overhead rate.

◆ *All costs.* Even though direct and overhead costs include almost all costs, this fee would generally be higher and cover long-term costs incurred by the organization. For your sports camp, it would cover all costs plus wear and tear on the building, long-term marketing, establishing a reserve fund, etc.

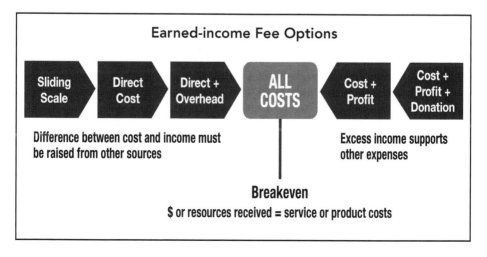

◆ *Breakeven.* A price that allows a nonprofit to cover exactly
all costs associated with a program or service. Revenues less
expenses equals zero.

◆ *Cost + profit.* This fee is based on all costs of the program, plus a
small amount toward other nonprofit needs. If you are a parent,
you probably encountered field trip forms with this message.
"The field trip is twelve dollars. Two dollars of your fee is to
provide a scholarship to a child who would not be able to attend
without your support." This also occurs when you set a price
based on selling 85 percent of the seats, but then sell out.

◆ *Cost + profit + donation.* This fee includes all of your costs, plus
a donation to your nonprofit. From the perspective of this book,
this fee is a combination of mission income and individual
donations. A nonprofit uses this pricing structure for events that
regularly sell out.

Memberships

Finally, no discussion of mission income would be complete without a
brief membership discussion. Where do memberships fit? Are they earned

---

Get More Income from Your Membership

Erick Lindblad, CEO of the Sanibel-Captiva Conservation Foundation,
learned something valuable about membership. Several years ago,
the foundation decided to separate its membership and annual giving
efforts. The most important result of this separation was a great increase
in individual donations. While membership numbers and income from it
remained roughly the same after the split, the funds generated by the
annual campaign grew by more than 25 percent. Lindblad credits this
success to the opportunity the split offered to tell two distinct stories.
The first story was about membership and its benefits. The second
was about being a donor and donor benefits. Each story fulfilled two
different needs and provided value to two different audiences.

income or individual fundraising? While many nonprofits invite people to become members with the hope that they will become donors, this is unlikely. In my opinion, memberships are mission-income opportunities. They engage individuals who seek to participate in your mission and belong. In contrast, individual fundraising is about giving a donation with the rewards that donations bring, such as giving back, meeting important basic human needs, helping those with less, and bringing about change.

Memberships often include inducements, such as free entry, key chains, and advance announcements. When you squish membership and donations together, you perplex people who care about you. You also lose income.

To Recap

◆ Mission is the heart of your nonprofit. Money is its fuel. Mission-income success combines heart and fuel together.

◆ Mission income is the biggest of the three main sources of nonprofit income.

◆ The benefits of mission income include independence, closeness to customers, sustainability, efficiency, and the possibility that your services will be of more value than ever.

◆ The challenges with mission income include the possibility that collecting it will conflict with beliefs about your work, you may need to make cultural changes, it may be hard to find viable ideas, you may need new skills, and you might confuse your donors.

Chapter Two

Stream Two—Individual Giving

IN THIS CHAPTER

···→ Individual Giving

···→ Individual Giving and Groups

···→ Individual Giving of Major Gifts and Bequests

Since individual donations are the most complex of all nonprofit income streams, this chapter is divided into three sections. The first section focuses on individual giving, the second section on creating groups of donors, and the third on major gifts, including bequests.

We are surrounded by extraordinary events so common, we often fail to appreciate them. Consider the following:

◆ Homeless men with mental illness receive dental care. A donor who lives in a $1 million condominium pays for the dental services.

◆ People across the world gather to hear world-class music performed by live orchestras, a feat that was once solely the prerogative of royalty. Donors from the local community fund the performances.

◆ Children receive free tutoring. Some of the funds paying for it were donated by people who died before the children's parents were born.

What makes these occasions so extraordinary? Individual donors create them. Individuals voluntarily give resources they might use elsewhere to support the work of nonprofit organizations. These extraordinary everyday miracles are the core of individual giving. A person donates funds to your organization for which the donor receives no direct service. Please understand: This is not to say donors receive no benefits, but the majority of the direct benefits go to third parties. Donors' benefits are *tokens*, or *intangible*.

> ### Individual Donation
>
> Gifts given by individuals and families to nonprofit organizations. The individual donation may include nominal contributions; major gifts of $20,000, $100,000, or more; a gift of millions left by a philanthropist through a bequest; and everything in between.
>
>
> **definition**

This chapter explores individual donations, one of the seven nonprofit income streams, and summarizes oodles of materials to provide you with an overview of how nonprofits engage and inspire people to donate. Finally, while I believe every nonprofit can benefit from donations, this book can help you decide what role individual donations will play in your nonprofit's income strategy. To help, I have condensed the benefits and drawbacks of individual giving.

Why Do People Donate Hard-Earned Money to Nonprofit Organizations?

I asked a group at a meeting of the Association of Fundraising Professionals this question. The attendees gave excellent answers. "They care about our cause." "They believe in us." "They will get a tax deduction."

Fortunately, for everyone seeking donations, social scientists have studied the "whys" of giving. As shared by Larry Johnson in *The Eight Principles of Sustainable Fundraising*, The Center on Philanthropy at Indiana University identified these five individual gift motivators:

1. To meet important basic human needs

2. To give back

3. To help those with less

4. To bring about a desired change

5. Because they were asked

If you intend to earn lots of individual donations, do not just use these phrases—see them as practical tools in your pursuit of this income. You will thereby help potential donors learn how you can help them meet basic needs, give back, share with those who have less, and create desired impacts. You will also ask individuals for donations.

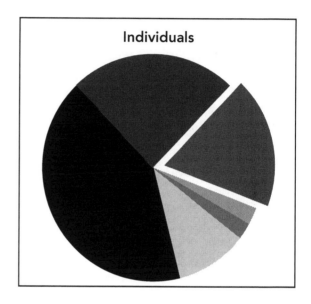

Individual donations, along with mission income and government funds, represent the three big players in nonprofit income. Donations are gifts and not earned income. Nonetheless, you will work to win them.

From the Nonprofit's Viewpoint, What Is the Individual Giving Process Like?

When I begin a journey, I find it helpful to look at a big map of the geographic area I plan to cover. Similarly, this section provides the big picture on how nonprofits win individual donations as a major revenue source.

1. Identify, Invite, and Communicate

To start individual fundraising in a nonprofit, you develop a list of supporters. On it, you include volunteers, staff, your alumni, current customers, people who have donated to you online, and others who have a connection to the nonprofit. If you don't have a list and you wish to obtain individual donations, begin one today. Continue collecting names for the rest of your nonprofit's life or until you have too much money. (I haven't seen that happen yet!) Besides individual names, collect mailing addresses, emails, and permission to stay in contact. Other information about these prospects is helpful, such as your connections with them and their workplaces, interests, and hobbies—and especially why your mission interests them. For example, a prospect loves dogs, and your nonprofit's mission is to care for abused dogs. Record this information in a database designed for donor information.

As you meet people, encourage them to establish closer relationships with your organization. To do this, you offer events, visits, newsletter, calls, coffee dates, or an endless swath of casual or formal—but intentional—interactions. Mike Mansfield, a CEO with a Habitat for Humanity affiliate, calls these opportunities "on-ramps." Again, your nonprofit will continue offering engagement opportunities forever.

The Big Guys

Individual donations, along with mission income and government funds, represent the three big players in nonprofit income. Donations are gifts and not earned income. Nonetheless, you will work to win them.

principle

Communicate frequently. In addition to offering invitations to events, you share stories of your nonprofit's successes and educate people about your mission. You also share how individuals can help further the mission with in-kind gifts and donations. You explain how donations help and how you use them to solve basic needs and change lives. You let individuals know what each gift will buy and why gifts are needed—and that no gift is too small.

2. Request and Respond

The second step of the individual donation process is requesting funds and responding when you receive them. While you might have done this casually in the past, now you become more intentional. Whether a donor gives $10 or $10,000, you respond with thanks and appreciation, because of the following:

◆ You are grateful.

◆ Gifts are always optional, and the gift might represent a sacrifice.

◆ The gift might be to test the donor's experience at your organization, and it could be a prelude to more gifts.

◆ The gift could have been given to a different cause.

◆ The cost per dollar to obtain future donations is low compared with other nonprofit income streams.

Your systematic requests for more donations start with those closest to you. For example, board members ask other board members for gifts.

You follow this up by mailing an appeal letter requesting a donation from every person on your list. This is an investment because this is how you find your new donors, some of whom will give you major gifts justifying your long-term mindset. Typically, initial appeals fail to return the costs of sending them and are considered a long-term investment with the goal of identifying donors. Most direct-mail experts say that if all goes well, your first mail appeal will cover its costs and break even. If you select individual donations to be a major source of your income again, you will ask for donations, in some variation, forever. Some supporters will give, some won't, and some will give more than asked.

3. Stewardship

From our satellite viewpoint, you identified a small group of donors. To keep them, you "steward" them. Here, stewardship means to love, care for, and respect all donors. In part, this is sharing your gratitude, expressing how their gifts have helped, how they served those whom they intended to help, and how they made a difference.

Stewardship is an often-overlooked part of the individual giving process. It involves much more than just posting a thank-you note, even though gift acknowledgment is vital. Besides gratitude, stewardship shows donors how else they might engage in your nonprofit's work. For instance, you invite one donor to review an article before publication. You invite another to meet with artists being considered for an exhibit. You ask a

Creating a Culture of Income Plenty

I interviewed Dr. Kumar Mahadevan, president of Mote Marine Laboratory and Aquarium, on a damp, overcast day in January. During his thirty-five-year tenure, Mahadevan saw Mote, whose mission promotes today's research for tomorrow's oceans, grow from a small research lab into a major institution. If your nonprofit is interested in individual donations, Mote is a great example of what dedication to obtaining individual donations means and how it can shape an institution. Following is an excerpt from our conversation.

Q: Over the years, what has been the hardest income to raise at Mote?
A: Individual donations. Every year, donations start at zero. Obtaining them depends in part on the economy. Unfortunately, only a sliver of all donors are interested in marine research. Mote faces lots of competition for dollars from nonprofits, especially those promoting social causes. Unlike the universities with whom Mote competes for funding, we lack a huge, dedicated alumni.

Q: If they are such a challenge, why continue to seek donations?
A: In the late 1970s, we realized that to fund research, we needed individual donors. Research grants only fund part of the need for every project. Since Mote wanted to continue to do research, we needed funding from outside the research community.

Q: How did you do it?
A: We looked for ways to engage the local community. We started by focusing on youth and started a science education component and summer camps for children. In the 1980s, to reach more people, we opened the aquarium. At first, the aquarium was what I jokingly called "a glorified pet shop." Now, it provides over $1 million in operating support. Next, we opened a state-of-the-art shark tank that drew 22,000 visitors and created great buzz. Recently, when we noticed that our local donor base had flattened, we considered how else we might reach out to find more donors. We now bring in traveling live exhibits, such as sea lions.

Q: You took a long-term view and stuck with your strategy. Did this also provide other benefits besides donations?
A: Yes, our volunteer force grew from a handful of people to over 1,300 people today. Volunteers contribute more than 200,000 hours annually. Today, Mote has more than 10,500 individual members and 130 corporate partners.

stories from the real world

third to help you select a roofing contractor. Stewardship is about helping donors become engaged as partners in your work. Stewardship continues forever. Over time, you recognize that some people donate and help your organization more than others, and you act on this knowledge. To continue to grow donations, you focus on individuals who have access to lots of resources, who have great connections, and who are street savvy—all of which will help your nonprofit with money and more. In time, you find the 10 percent who do 90 percent of the heavy individual gift giving.

4. Culture Change

Staff and other leaders eventually improve how they ask for money. They had better clarify why individual donor support is needed and how it will help. Likewise, because money follows mission, your nonprofit improves its services, including the quality of its theatrical performances, its land management, or whatever. Everyone grows in confidence. This invites donations.

A culture of philanthropy is beginning. This culture includes a widely shared attitude that everyone needs to play a philanthropic part at whatever level the individual can afford. It includes a recognition that you offer something unique and with great value. Board, staff, and volunteers become part of the effort. In turn, current supporters invite new donors to share in the privilege of doing meaningful work. Over time, you realize that you stand in a field of plenty and that your requests for donations are truly generous offers to share the wealth that your mission offers.

5. Select and Study

Once again, from our thirty-thousand-foot viewpoint, when we look at the individual fundraising process, we recognize a focus on major gifts. The staff studies donor lists to identify people with commitment, connection, and the means to make such gifts. These individuals receive special handling.

For instance, a CEO invites a donor for lunch to learn the donor's specific goals. During lunch, they discuss how the nonprofit might help the donor achieve these goals. After lunch, the CEO sends a thank-you note and suggests the next steps to move the goals forward.

Selecting and studying donors is a prelude to a request for major funds. Each nonprofit defines what amount equals a major gift. This amount changes over time, ideally growing larger as the nonprofit grows.

Furthermore, this process of selecting individuals from whom to request major gifts is an example of prospect research. Prospect research can be casual, such as when you look up the online value of someone's home. Or it can be extensive. For example, your nonprofit might hire an expert to collect publicly available data on twenty-five of your best prospects. "When you believe you have the potential to secure annual gifts or multiyear pledges of $10,000 or more," advises prospect research expert Jen Filla with Aspire Research Group, "it's time to invest in prospect research to avoid leaving money on the table and to find opportunities to make giving more appealing."

6. *Target, Ready, Aim, Fire*

Actually asking for a major gift often takes place in the privacy of the donor's home. Here, your organization's key leaders personally ask an individual or couple to make a gift. Drumroll, please. After what seems like a long period of silence in which the person asking for the donation remains silent, the donor answers yes or says, "We want to talk this over." Or perhaps the couple smiles and one of them replies, "No, thanks." Like the earlier steps, the process continues forever.

There you have it—the individual fundraising process in six steps. Does it always work like this? Yes. If you focus on process, increase your skills in individual fundraising, and continue following the process. Individual donors, of course, create their own path. Few follow this six-step process exactly. Some donors go straight to major gifts. Others continue to make annual gifts, no matter the efforts to increase the donation. Others donate for a year or two and then disappear.

Overall, using the process to raise funds from individuals requires the following:

- ◆ Focus

- ◆ Consistency

- ◆ Time

- ◆ Skills

Is individual fundraising really a mystery? No. It is hard, long-term—yet rewarding—work.

Are Individual Donations a Major Funding Stream for Your Nonprofit?

Each nonprofit funding stream has benefits and challenges. Individual donations, while perennially popular, are no different. In this section, you will learn the five major benefits of individual donations—besides money. These are followed by four major challenges. As you read, consider if the benefits outweigh the challenges for your nonprofit.

Benefits

No Gift Too Small

One key benefit of individual donations is that everyone can participate. No donation is too small. Donations represent people who support

---

Mystery No More

One goal of this book is to help you take the mystery out of obtaining nonprofit income. Of all the sources, individual donations entail the most mystery. To remove some of it, consider these truths: numbers, art, and science.

◆ **Numbers.** Generating individual donations is a numbers game. To receive individual donations, you will work with a lot of people. Many will not donate, but some will.

◆ **Art.** Acquiring individual gifts is an art based on relationship building. It is filled with surprises that delight and disappoint. No one knows in advance if any individual will donate.

◆ **Science.** Individual giving also is a science. Proven methods exist. Understanding how people behave collectively helps predict your results. If you ask consistently, improve how and who you ask, and likewise improve your mission work, your nonprofit will succeed.

What is the biggest challenge with individual fundraising? Resilience. What are the benefits of not giving up? Finding what motivates people to give to your nonprofit and engaging them in your work. You can do it.

you. The more supporters you have, the more mission you can do. This ability to gather individuals who care about your work is an important asset.

Every successful nonprofit needs a community of support. The availability of a constituency you can call to action is one of the tools you use to bring about your vision. Besides money, a community of support that champions the cause, attends events, and cheers enthusiastically when your name is mentioned is invaluable.

Habitat for Humanity supporters show up on Saturday mornings with hammers in hand. They stand at zoning committee meetings. And they make donations. You can't do it alone. Individual donors prove you're a community.

Fewer Hoops per Dollar

Compared with other forms of nonprofit income, the process of obtaining individual donors is straightforward. Once the money is given, you encounter fewer strings, hoops, and barriers to wiggle around, jump through, and cross before you can spend it.

Obtaining individual donations is neither simple nor easy, but compared with other income streams, once you have a process under way, earning money takes less effort per dollar.

Passion to the People

Parents of children at your school, opera lovers who attend your performances, and enthusiasts who hike your trails are all people who understand your value. They want your mission to continue. They are also the people most likely to donate. As part of your community, they will shape your work in desirable ways.

For instance, they might suggest an improvement to which they contribute and solicit others to fund. They recommend event speakers—whom they will contact and house.

Passionate supporters hold the potential to truly enhance your efforts and make your vision come true.

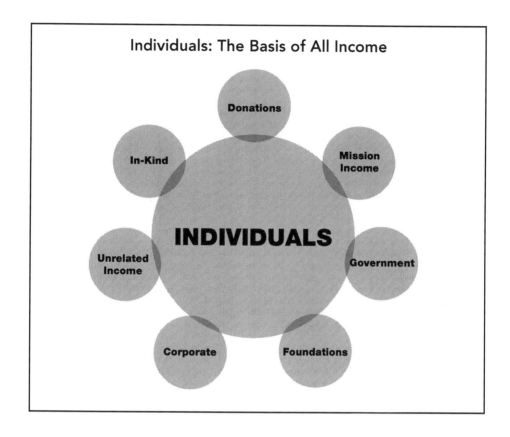

Ultimately, Individuals Control Money

Seeking individual donations and gaining relationship skills strengthen a nonprofit's understanding of all the potential income streams. Ultimately, an individual signs every check or credit card receipt whether the individual represents a foundation, a corporation, a government, or self. All income results from an individual deciding to obtain value from your nonprofit. As illustrated, as you grow in your understanding of individual giving, your skills for obtaining all kinds of nonprofit income will grow.

Unique to Nonprofits

As a nonprofit, you can accept donations. In return, people can receive tax benefits for making them. While studies show that tax benefits are not extreme motivators of individual donations, gift deductibility, nonetheless, is a unique nonprofit benefit offered to donors.

Why People Are Reluctant to Pursue Individual Donations and Suggested Solutions

Challenges

With all the benefits, it might seem that every nonprofit will actively pursue individual donations. You will have competition for individual donations, but less than you expect because of these challenges:

Fear of Rejection

Most people avoid being turned down. While rejection from a local foundation is painful, the sting is not as sharp or as awkward as the rest of the meeting with the donor who shouts that you have a lot of gall asking for money. (Or whatever nightmare you conjure in your mind.) To overcome this fear, rethink it. Your interactions with potential donors are a chance to find someone who shares your passion and is willing to back that passion with monetary action. You have so many amazing people to meet, to know, and to ask.

Stereotyping Solicitors

Dinner is on the table, piping hot. Calm settles over your household. You lift your fork to taste your meatball, and the telephone rings. It's a #!@!## solicitor. We've all been asked to donate at inappropriate times in inappropriate ways. Everyone detests these intrusions. Even though statistics show that, done right, the telephone can be more effective than mail, I personally believe that this method leaves a residue of resentment. In my opinion, good individual donations are solicited by mail, in groups, and in face-to-face meetings organized to discuss the donor's interests and the nonprofit's needs. When done well, funding requests do not interrupt dinner.

It's Hard Work

Successful individual fundraising requires nurturing, discipline, self-growth, and patience. To succeed, you will work hard. Some days, you will ask for money and receive none. Other days, you will ask for money and receive some. Sometimes you will work long and hard to cultivate a donor, and the gift amount will not meet your expectations. Along the way, you *will* have amazing success. It's like Candy Land. If you play long enough, you *will* get to the candy.

Lack of Focus

Many nonprofits lack clarity on how to obtain individual donations. They experiment with different techniques, have poor discipline, and prefer what is comfortable to interacting with donors who intimidate them. Lacking focus is like using a plastic sandbox shovel to dig into hard ground. What you need is a heavy-duty steel garden spade. While you will make headway with the plastic shovel, it will break a lot and you will have to frequently start and stop. Successful individual fundraising is a process where you succeed by investing in focused, disciplined efforts.

Because of these challenges and more, the competition for people who share a passion for your cause will be small. To learn more about individual donations, read the next two sections. If you believe that individual donations will be only a minor source of income at your nonprofit, you may want to skip ahead to Chapter Three: Stream Three—Government Funding.

Individual Giving and Groups

One Monday morning, Mike Mansfield, development director at a Habitat for Humanity affiliate, received a telephone call. A man, we'll call him Joe, introduced himself: "We had a few friends over last night. Everyone put a check in a bowl for Habitat. It totals about $20,000. Would you like to come over and pick them up?"

Naturally, Mike said yes. Instead of a quick visit to Joe's upscale community, Mike took time to get to know Joe. During the conversation, Mike learned all about Joe's interests and the event that triggered his call. Joe, it turned out, had a passion for Habitat. He was eager to help. Mike shared that if Joe and his friends were interested, they could sponsor a house for $50,000.

Joe was interested. With Habitat's support, Joe developed a steering committee composed of like-minded friends. In a few months, the committee launched the first of what became an annual golf tournament. Year one, it raised funds to build one house and drew 120 volunteers. In five years, the group raised enough money to build seven houses and was challenging other upscale communities with fundraising contests. In time, the community where Joe lived became the source of over $1 million in donations for Habitat.

"It was all about their relationships," Mike shared. "It would have taken me years to meet all those people. With Joe's help, I helped him and his friends make a meaningful contribution. They thanked me as much as I thanked them."

When it comes to raising individual donations, developing groups of motivated donors can offer your nonprofit tremendous benefits. Although the one-on-one aspects of individual fundraising must never be ignored, the good news is that a lot of individual fundraising effort can be implemented in groups. This section focuses on the group aspect of individual donations. It provides a big-picture overview and invites you to think about how to use group activities as tools to create donors with passion for your work.

Why are groups important? Groups of people are the means to create and sustain the changes that most nonprofits seek. While its authorship is uncertain, the following quote attributed to Margaret Mead sums it up nicely: "Never doubt that a small group of thoughtful, committed citizens can change the world. Indeed, it is the only thing that ever has."

While great leaders inspire and lead, supporters do the work of change. And the more supporters you have, the more power you have to create change. For example, the British slave system had enormous economic value and yielded tremendous power, yet British slavery ended in large part because of grassroots efforts, including boycotts of slave-grown sugar.

The previous section explored the individual giving process. Section two centers on creating groups of donors.

First: The Big House Group

Good news! Even if you have never received a donation, you already have a group of potential donors. I call this first group your Big House Group. This reflects its central importance to your endeavor to earn individual donations. "Big house" refers to the estate culture of Georgian England. In small villages, the big house or estate was a key economic unit in the village. It was surrounded by smaller homes and businesses that succeeded because of the existence of the big house. Your Big House Group is that important.

Your Big House Group includes your key leaders, board, staff, and volunteers. To make individual donations a major part of your nonprofit income stream, you start here. This is sometimes the most uncomfortable place for people to begin. Why? For most of us, it is easier to hope that Mrs. Bigbucks will give us money than it is to ask the sweet person who volunteers at your front desk each week to do even more for the mission by making a cash donation. Asking your volunteer might, however, be easier than asking your staff for donations when they haven't had a raise in three years. Yet these people have the most devotion to your cause, most clearly recognize the critical need for cash, and understand what that cash means for your mission. What's more, they are the people who, with their gifts, will inspire others to give. They are the people expected by other donors (those not in the Big House Group) to donate first.

In many, many ways, succeeding with individual donations is about courage. Gathering courage to ask someone to make a huge gift is one type of courage. Gathering courage to put your own cash in the bowl is another. Another type of courage challenges people to commit time and dollars to your organization and the mission it represents. In short, this courage is about seeing what you really offer and the opportunity to belong to something larger than the individual donor. Success takes these kinds of courage and a belief in your work.

The people closest to your work are the ones who have the most faith in it. They witness your faults, see you overcoming adversity, yet remain true. In short, they must give because, to repeat an oft-asked question, "Why would someone who hardly knows you have more faith in your organization than the people closest to it?"

The graphic above shows concentric circles that trace where giving starts and who is most likely to donate to your nonprofit. It starts with your commitment and your gift. From here, it moves to those closest to your mission—your key leaders, then to other board members and staff. Next, you seek funds from volunteers and others who regularly participate to make your mission happen, including referral partners. After this, you invite friends and contacts of everyone already making gifts to participate. You include customers, customers' families, and neighbors who see your work. Returning to the big house metaphor, these are people who know about the manor and interact with it on occasion. In the most distant circle are the people who may have an interest and passion for your cause but

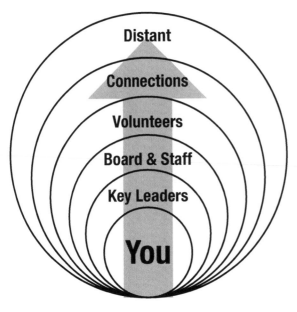

don't know about your work. They have passion and means but, as of yet, no connection. For example, donors who give to a cause like yours in distant cities. After you contact everyone closer in, you can begin to think of strategies to reach these passionate people you don't know.

Just like you, your acquaintances and donors have relationships with other people. Some represent mutual acquaintances; most differ. Your donors, for instance, have different neighbors, business acquaintances, and relatives. When you find people with a passion for your cause, many—if you help them as Mike did with Joe—will ask their friends, family, and colleagues to support your cause.

The big house metaphor is about the origin of donors, not dollars raised. The big house reminds us that the sure path to lots of donations, some of them major, begins from within and moves from there to friends, acquaintances, and finally strangers.

So far, we have used the concept of the big house to learn where you will find your biggest group of donors. Since obtaining individual donations is an ongoing process, the next segment discusses the kind of culture that nonprofits create to support ongoing individual donations as a major income stream over multiple years. This is called a culture of philanthropy.

A Culture of Philanthropy

What is a culture of philanthropy like in practice? Julie is a children's therapist at Easter Seals. She is not part of the development staff, but she understands that donations make a world of difference at Easter Seals. While she provides therapy to children, she comes into daily contact with many parents. One day, a new mother told Julie that her husband was a prestigious lawyer with clients across the country. At the next session, Julie learned that the family had recently moved to the area in part because of the services this Easter Seals offered. Julie listened and heard. She arranged for the mother to meet the development director the next time her child had an appointment. In response to the mother's interests and desire to meet others, the development director invited the mother to join the communications committee. Later that year, the family gave $1,000 as part of the annual appeal. A year later, they gave $5,000. In three years, the mother served on the board and the family gave the first of many annual gifts of $10,000. Because she works in a culture of philanthropy, Julie understands that she can help Easter Seals to have the resources children need. She does this by paying attention to what she hears and sharing it with the appropriate person—in this case, her development director.

To successfully make individual giving a major income source, develop a culture of philanthropy. Its modus operandi is that everyone who surrounds your nonprofit understands the need for philanthropy, makes gifts themselves, and is comfortable talking about it and suggesting that others give. Fundraising, therefore, is group based. It is not the responsibility of the CEO or development staff. It's a team effort, where the development staff and CEO become the team captains who organize the effort.

How can you nurture a culture of philanthropy? The following list outlines the steps and thinking needed to begin.

Commit to Individual Fundraising and Create a Supportive Culture

Creating a culture of philanthropy begins with deciding to make individual donations a major funding stream. This commitment results from strategic work at the board and leadership levels. The strategic thinking might go like this: "We are a nonprofit that receives cash

> ### You Have to Fundraise... Even If You Don't!
>
> *Even if you don't have to fundraise, you need to fundraise. It improves your public image and helps you to build relationships.*
>
> —Erick Lindblad, CEO, Sanibel-Captiva Conservation Foundation

donations from those nearest and dearest to us." Commitment requires follow-up actions.

Start with You

To start a culture of philanthropy at your nonprofit right now, reach for your wallet. Pull out a bill. Insert it in an envelope. Give it to your fiscal person as a donation. I am talking about you, the reader. *Really, I mean you.*

Think Like a Donor Educator

A culture of philanthropy sounds lovely in the abstract. To create one, you must commit to ongoing education about the benefits of philanthropy and its value to the work of your nonprofit. Again, start with yourself (reading this counts). Along with education comes assessment. Where are the people involved with your nonprofit in terms of understanding the requirements of individual fundraising and how it works? Do they expect you to ask them for donations? What information do they have about how you are funded? Do they understand why you decided to make individual donations one of your key funding streams? In any nonprofit that expects individual donations to be a major funding stream, donor education is an ongoing need. This is because people are always leaving and new people are arriving. It's also because people forget. Donors, like everyone else, are bombarded daily with messages. If you want people to be aware of opportunities and even begin to ask others to support the mission, they need to understand why and how they can help.

Leaders Next

A culture of philanthropy is like a great party where the hosts arrive first and set the tone for the evening. Who are your hosts? First, establish a firm deadline for when you will ask all your leaders for a gift. Then, as discussed in the "big house" section, include your CEO and board chair. Next add the executive committee, the staff management team, and the other board members. After you ask these leaders and help them ask each other, you ask everyone in some way connected with your nonprofit for an individual donation. In a culture of philanthropy, the language of leadership reflects the expectation that they will be asked and that people who are serious about the mission's work will participate in a meaningful way—that is, not the least they can do, but the most.

Key Players

To develop further a culture of philanthropy after the leaders contribute, systematically ask for donations from other staff, volunteers, and people otherwise connected with your nonprofit. However, before you raise funds, in most cases, you need to raise friends. That is, get a chance to know them and offer them the chance to know you. Consider how interactive experiences such as special events, educational programs, and meetings might help you meet people and help them get to know your nonprofit's work. For instance, a film festival offers parties with film themes. A small

---

Will This Be Easy?

Individual fundraising is hard. It's hard to get people to meet with you. It's hard to get them to tour your site, but when they do it's always so meaningful. And it changes everything.

—Martha Macris, Executive Director, Memorial Assistance Ministries, Houston

❝ ❞

Find a Way

Danny sought funds to develop several teaching films. Together we identified a handful of key supporters who we believed could write checks. They knew Danny's nonprofit's work, the importance of the films—and they shared his passion. All had already dedicated hundreds of hours to the film project. The first person Danny asked was a retired professor. Danny asked for $500 to help finish a film. The professor said he didn't have the money. The second person interrupted Danny in the middle of the request. He refused to listen to it. Instead, he gave Danny three alternative funding sources to pursue.

Danny was disheartened. After grieving, he pursued the three new sources. In the meantime, the retired professor emailed to say that he had an opportunity to do a special lecture and that he would dedicate the money earned to the film. Within sixty days, Danny obtained the funds he needed, and he learned a great deal about individual giving.

 stories from the real world

college holds lectures and invites alumni and people with multiple degrees to showcase the college's contributions to local intellectual life. Group activities are an ideal way to cultivate many people at once.

Furthermore, in a culture of philanthropy, conversations about giving become part of the everyday language of the nonprofit. Even if a new staff member is terrified of asking for a gift, with support and education, most can become comfortable expressing appreciation for donors and helping people understand that the organization is supported through donations.

Along the way, your supporters will do some of your work for you. They will create friendships with others and invite them to help. Over time, people will not only want to support your work, but they will also want to be with the other people who also believe your work is important. This interactive dividend is one of key values of special events, whether a gala, education event, or something in between. Some people will form new friendships, others new professional connections. Still others will bond over your cause. Newcomers, for example, gravitate to Sarasota's Florida Winefest & Auction event because it is a great way to meet other newcomers and support local children.

Just Ask Everybody—Not!

Unfortunately, even in a culture of philanthropy, no one has the time or energy to ask everyone in the world to support you. Just as singles go to places to meet other singles, nonprofits in a culture of philanthropy put more focus on people with the ability to help the most. In essence, this involves people like Julie at Easter Seals, being keenly aware of potential donors

People Who Won't Play

What if you have a board, staff, or others who, despite your patient efforts to educate them, still refuse to make individual donations? Can you still make individual donations a major funding stream for your nonprofit? Yes, but it will be more challenging. Just as a person who is blind can run a five-kilometer race against sighted individuals, you will need to take a long view and plan your actions accordingly. Over time, work to decrease the number of board and staff members who can participate but won't, especially in leadership positions. Do not wait for everybody to get on board. In short, if it's the right income strategy for the nonprofit, move on your vision and find new supporters soon.

observation

who would make natural philanthropists and creating opportunities for them. The team captains coordinate where to focus efforts to obtain major and planned gifts, which is the focus of the next section.

Changing any culture is difficult. To avoid an all-hands-on-deck effort, some nonprofits decide to limit development to one individual. While this approach can work, it means that the nonprofit is always one heartbeat away from a funding crisis. A culture of philanthropy, while difficult to create and sustain, is a great way to create stable income in a nonprofit. It has the benefit of building a community of support that can provide knowledge, insight, wisdom—and money.

As the book of Ecclesiastes reminds us in the Bible, "Two are better than one, because they have a good return for their labor: If either of them falls down, one can help the other up. But pity anyone who falls and has no one to help them up. Also, if two lie down together, they will keep warm. But how can one keep warm alone? Though one may be overpowered, two can defend themselves. A cord of three strands is not quickly broken."

Individual Giving of Major Gifts and Bequests

Harvard University has 323,000 living alumni. With individual fundraising, Harvard's challenge is not a lack of interested prospects. The challenge is to separate alumni who will donate, with reasonable levels of encouragement, from those who won't. Its challenge is to identify philanthropic alumni with means and passion who will make *major* gifts, which at Harvard's Graduate School of Education begin at $50,000. Identifying who to ask and helping them invest in your nonprofit is the heart of obtaining large gifts from individuals and is the focus of this section.

To whet your appetite for major, planned, and bequest gifts, here are some tantalizing statistics:

◆ Fewer than 20 percent of donors give 80 percent of the money to nonprofits.

◆ A typical planned gift is two hundred to three hundred times the size of a donor's annual gift.

◆ Bequests average over $65,000, and donors who give bequests are "shy" about revealing these gifts. Only one in seven will reveal their intent.

Triple Play

This is the third and final section on individual giving, one of seven nonprofit income streams. In the first individual giving section, you learned about the benefits of individual gifts. Then in the following section, you discovered how nonprofits work with groups to obtain individual gifts. In this section, the goal is to help you begin to identify the 20 percent who will give 80 percent of the donations and to encourage, invite, and nurture them to invest.

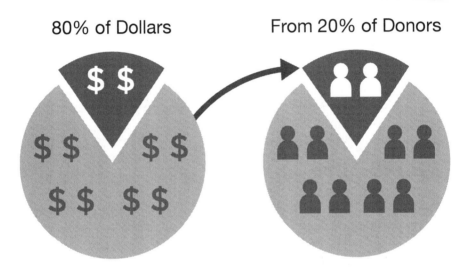

What can your nonprofit do to create these large gifts? Focus on actions you control. Success comes to nonprofits that engage involved individuals, usually current supporters, to invest in their future.

While you will always leave the side doors open to the unsought major gifts, focus on lighting up your front porch, laying out a welcome mat, and inviting friends to join you. To obtain major gifts, nonprofits identify potential donors, study their interests, develop opportunities based on those interests, and ask for the gifts so value can accrue to the donor, the nonprofit, and the mission it serves.

Working Vocabulary

To help you explore major gifts, this section examines three basic ideas. While a major gift vocabulary list can extend to several pages, the intention here is to give you a general idea of several concepts to increase your major-gift comfort level.

What Is a Major Gift?

A major gift is one that makes everyone at your nonprofit excited. Every nonprofit determines its own definition of major gift, and it often changes over time. For startups, a major gift is often that first gift greater than $5,000. While the money is super, it importantly demonstrates that a donor believes in your work. For some nonprofits, a gift must exceed $10,000, $100,000, or $1 million to be considered major. In one $25 million capital campaign, a Canadian hospital set a gift level of $100,000 as the minimum requirement for a donor to be appointed to the steering committee.

What Is a Planned Gift?

Planned gifts are gifts that involve preplanning, which also may be called gift planning. Generally, these include gifts of an individual's assets instead of current income, such as one hundred shares of stock. The "planning" can be extensive and include meeting with an attorney, financial advisor, accountant, and nonprofit staff. It can also be simple. On a life insurance beneficiary form, a donor lists your nonprofit. Bequests are the most common planned gifts by far.

What Is a Bequest?

A bequest is an individual gift given to your nonprofit through a donor's estate or will. When your nonprofit

---

The Lucky Break That's Unlucky

Sometime during your individual fundraising journey you will get a lucky break. Perhaps it's a surprise gift of $10,000, $100,000, or even $1 million. Unfortunately, unpredictable and unrepeatable windfalls like these are rare. The odds are that you won't *ever* be lucky in the same way again. Yet many nonprofits spend needless energy, time, and money trying to recreate them. When windfalls arrive, celebrate. Then return to your tried-and-true processes to obtain major gifts. As the professor tells the children in *The Lion, The Witch, and The Wardrobe*, "You won't get to Narnia that way again."

watch out!

is named in a will, a lawyer will contact the nonprofit. This does not mean that you will receive funds. Estate gifts are made only once the individual's obligations have been paid.

Planned giving, a subgroup of major gifts, includes a bevy of financial tools such as CRATs. These tools help donors make charitable gifts, obtain tax advantages, take care of family matters—and, in some cases, receive income.

Unfortunately, these tools are so confusing that nonprofit leaders freeze when they contemplate discussing a CRUT, CRAT, or CLAT (see definition sidebar) with donors. This is the brain surgery of nonprofit income. Many nonprofits believe that because they don't understand how to use the

---

CRUT, CRAT, and CLAT

CRUT, or charitable remainder unitrust, is a type of trust where a donor irrevocably transfers assets to a nonprofit, which becomes the trustee. The nonprofit then invests the assets and pays the donor annual income from the asset's earnings. This income varies. At the donor's death, any remaining assets belong to the nonprofit.

CRAT, or charitable remainder annuity trust, is another type of trust. It is like a CRUT except that the donor receives a set amount of yearly income. This amount is agreed upon when the trust is established.

CLAT, or charitable lead annuity trust, is also an irrevocable trust. In this case, the trust pays a fixed amount of income to the nonprofit for a number of years or while the donor lives. When the term ends, any remaining assets are distributed to the donor or the donor's heirs.

---

instruments, they cannot obtain planned gifts. You do not need to know how to execute the particulars. In fact, you would be ill-advised to execute these instruments without expert advice. You do need to know that these instruments exist, and to be willing to encourage any interested donors to avail themselves of experts. Here is a summary of what you need to know and do:

◆ Understand that planned giving tools are instruments used by specialists. Gain a working knowledge of the tools, such as CRUTs, by reading books on the subject or attending Planned

Giving Council workshops or similar opportunities. Here you will learn about the tools and meet the people who frequently use them.

◆ Develop a team of on-call advisors. Include financial planners, estate and tax lawyers, and accountants. Alternately, work with your community foundation and access its staff, with the understanding that the foundation will manage some or all of the funds. While most donors will use their own advisors, refer them to your team as appropriate.

◆ Memorize this, or a similar statement, adapted from the work of Jack Miller, "If we can demonstrate a way to redirect your taxes to benefit your family, the community, and our mission, will you be willing to visit with me and an expert for half an hour to learn more?"

How Do Nonprofits Obtain Major Gifts?

Did you read about John Paulson's $100 million gift to the Central Park Conservancy? How did the conservancy obtain this gift? More importantly, how might your nonprofit obtain major gifts like it? The classic answer for any organization is that it found the following:

◆ The right person to ask

◆ The right reason to ask

◆ The right person to do the asking

◆ The right option of donating

◆ The right time to ask

This nonprofit maxim, when unraveled, makes several important points. The saying lists five required "rights." Getting these lined up is akin to hitting five birds with one stone. The adage suggests that obtaining major gifts doesn't happen every day, and it is not based on luck.

Of these rights, finding the right person is the biggest. The exact details of Paulson's decision and his interaction with the Central Park Conservancy might never be fully known, but we do know that Paulson had a deep family history with the park. It's where his grandparents held hands. As a small child, he was rolled through it in a carriage. At the time of the gift, Paulson regularly ran or cycled in the park. Besides the relationship, his net worth was estimated at $12.5 billion. Previously, he gave $20 million to NYU's Stern School of Business. Thus, Paulson had a deep connection to Central Park, had means, and was philanthropic. These criteria represent excellent standards for identifying potential major gift donors. Would you like another helpful criterion? It is this: The donor has given a previous gift to your nonprofit.

Knowing who to ask is still a long way from securing a major gift. Assuming you have an existing relationship with a potential donor, the next most important "right" is the right reason. Ideally, you determine a right reason for a gift in dialog with the potential donor. What are their interests? How would they like to be helped? Remembered? What are the organization's needs and dreams in this area? Where do the needs overlap with the interests? What might such an initiative cost?

Given all the "rights" that must be right, if the donor is not someone you have a strong existing relationship with, then identifying the right person who will do the asking is critical. Sally, a fellow consultant, made a $10,000 gift to Teach for America. She did so because a business associate invited her to a dinner to learn about the nonprofit. Since the associate had helped Sally and her husband a lot, Sally figured the dinner was about payback. What she learned was that she had an opportunity to help by sponsoring a classroom for a year and to touch the lives of all those little children. For Sally, the right person to ask was her business associate.

The right form of contributing is another of the rights. For instance, a gift may involve cash or other resources. Your donor responds positively when you suggest a gift of stock or property that provides tax benefits. A donor agrees to a large gift when you suggest tapping into an employee matching-gift program to double it. Your donor agrees to a gift given over three years rather than one made this year. Asking the right way is about helping donors find the best options for their finances and situations. Asking the right way involves offering options to transfer value that help donors meet their goals and needs.

The final "right" is the correct time. Beyond the obvious time conflicts, such as the day before a donor takes off for a cruise, the timing of the request is important. Few people make major gifts without some time for thinking and reflecting. Of course, the danger is that a prospect never finds the time. A bigger danger is waiting for the time to be perfect, which will never happen. By understanding the dynamics of patience, urgency, and knowing when to move on, the nonprofit leader is able to help donors fulfill their intentions and reap the benefits of making major gifts.

From Few to Many—Again

Up to this point, this section has explored winning big gifts by focusing on a few people in your community who have the means, passion, and connections. The rest of the section explores bequests. Bequests represent a notable exception to this narrow focus on a few individuals. To acquire bequests, your nonprofit concentrates on encouraging everyone to remember it in their estate plans.

Anyone Can Bequeath. Will You?

Imagine opening your mail and discovering a letter from an attorney informing you that your nonprofit is named in a will. Bequests form the biggest part of planned giving, equaling over 85 percent of all planned gifts. Gifts from estates provide an excellent way for individuals who

---

Where There's a Will...

Susan Ventura's favorite income is unrestricted major gifts. Ventura is the CEO of an Easter Seals affiliate. She prefers these funds because of their flexibility and ability to meet critical mission needs. Ventura's least favorite funds are service reimbursements that provide revenue to Easter Seals only when customers use services. In this case, Easter Seals must be staffed to provide them, even if people fail to keep appointments, which results in high expenses plus uncertain income.

Ventura's affiliate has moved away from big-gala-type special events. To promote individual fundraising, she prefers a small-group approach. This preference began when a volunteer in charge of the largest gala looked at the receipts and the work entailed and announced: "I can raise this much money by inviting dinner guests to my home." She did. After several years, the volunteer began to encourage her guests to hold events. The volunteer, with Ventura's help, took the idea of holding intimate events and franchised it, providing Easter Seals even more unrestricted revenue.

stories from
the real world

Growing Endowment

The Southeastern Guide Dogs endowment is growing by about $2 million per year. Approximately one hundred people have signed paperwork indicating that they have remembered the organization in their wills. Southeastern Guide Dogs' long-term goal is to have its endowment fund 50 percent of operations.

stories from the real world

care about your nonprofit to leave it a meaningful gift. Unfortunately, most people die without a will. Many nonprofits provide seminars to encourage those in their community to make one. From the long-term view, the opportunity to encourage people to create estate plans that both take care of their families and support your work represents an enormous opportunity for nonprofits.

Why are bequests attractive to donors? A bequest enables the person who fears running out of funds while living to ultimately contribute to your work. A bequest presents the donor with an ideal solution and the opportunity to make a contribution—if all works out well. It is inherently practical. By leaving money in the will to a beloved nonprofit, the nonprofit receives funds the deceased donor no longer needs. As a result, the bequest offers the nonprofit the opportunity to receive a major gift from a person of modest means.

Almost universally, nonprofits wish they had begun efforts to obtain bequests years ago, since it takes seven years on average to see results. Nonprofits can seek bequests as part of other income-development efforts. Every nonprofit can begin to ask people to remember them in their wills through existing publications. If you begin now and consistently pursue this form of giving, bequests can provide strong potential payoffs for little effort.

Since people make their estate plans at various trigger points in their own personal lives,

Sad, but True

Q: What is the biggest problem with a bequest?

A: It is the last gift you will receive from that donor.

observation

Is There a Shortcut?

Cliff Olstrom, executive director for over forty years with Tampa Lighthouse for the Blind, succeeds with bequests using a different approach. Instead of traditional individual fundraising, he followed this process:

Short term: Send mass mailings to new donors. The Lighthouse currently mails two or three appeals yearly to forty thousand households.

Long term: Create bequests. Place everyone who donates on the mailing list. Send newsletters several times yearly. Clearly communicate the need for and benefits of remembering the Lighthouse in estate plans.

What are the results? Approximately every other year, the Lighthouse receives a bequest. Most range from $10,000 to $200,000. In 1995, a donor provided $450,000.

While I can fill a stadium of fundraising specialists who will announce from the speakers that this approach is wrong, none will dispute the Lighthouse's success.

A more important question: Is this approach replicable? Here are key reasons it works:

◆ A population exists that is passionate about supporting people with vision challenges. The mass mailing sparks a response.

◆ The Lighthouse excels at keeping the spark alive with regular mailings. Potential donors learn that investing in the Lighthouse provides value.

◆ The Lighthouse receives excellent advice about mailing-list selections. The long-term approach allows the Lighthouse to fine-tune future mailings.

◆ The Lighthouse is consistent. This consistency required confidence, especially in the years before the strategy paid dividends.

What downsides exist? The Lighthouse forgoes other benefits from these donors, such as their wisdom, connections, and gifts while they live.

The Olstrom approach offers a strategy for nonprofits that don't plan to develop a traditional individual fundraising program while still seeking bequests.

stories from the real world

you must regularly and widely communicate a message about the mission's need. Even though you will encourage people, as part of your fundraising efforts, to share their plans, most donors, even with inducements, will never reveal their commitment. For nonprofits adopting individual gifts as a major funding stream, bequests and planned giving represents the ultimate individual donation. However, even if you choose not to focus on individual donations as a major income source, you can still obtain bequests by adopting a continual "remember-us-in-your-will" drip-marketing campaign. This campaign involves sending consistent, gentle reminders of the opportunity.

> ## Loving Affinity
>
> *The best indicator we have for planned gifts is affinity. Most nonprofits track giving. Anyone giving consecutively, especially five or more years, is a good candidate. Frequency is also an indicator. Those monthly donors? They think about your nonprofit every month. Special touches to those frequently giving individuals should bring serious planned-giving results.*
>
> —Jen Filla, Aspire Research Group
>
> **" "**

And here is one last bit of important information. Bequests also begin with *your own* personal gifts. While it might not be the right time to review your own will, you can designate a percentage of your pension or life insurance to your nonprofit by simply obtaining the beneficiary form and designating a specific dollar amount or percentage to your nonprofit. This act has symbolic significance. Consider it a rite of passage that announces to the world you are serious about obtaining major gifts.

To Recap

◆ Income from individual donors includes everything from the check your board member writes to special event revenue above and beyond the cost of the gala dinner to property you receive from an estate.

◆ People donate funds to nonprofits to meet important basic human needs, to give back, to help those with less, to bring about a desired change, and because they were asked.

◆ To obtain individual donations, identify, invite, and communicate with many people; request donations; "steward" donors; identify potential major donors; and request major donations.

◆ To make individual donations a major part of your nonprofit income stream, start with these groups: your board, staff, and volunteers.

◆ Obtaining major gifts is about focusing on the few to help them provide significant funding to a nonprofit. You prepare to work with and talk with major donors by developing individual fundraising efforts with many donors who teach you the ropes by giving you small donations.

◆ To obtain major gifts, nonprofits identify potential donors, study their interests, and develop donor-centric opportunities before asking for gifts.

◆ All nonprofits can obtain bequests. Bequests are the result of drip marketing consistently applied and encouraging those closest to the nonprofit, including your board, staff, and volunteers, to remember the nonprofit in their wills.

◆ Pursuing individual gifts as a major funding stream is not for the weak or fainthearted. It is the one income source of the seven streams that requires your nonprofit to listen most deeply to individuals in your community.

Chapter Three

Stream Three—Government Funding

IN THIS CHAPTER

···→ Grants, contracts, earmarks, and public-nonprofit partnerships

···→ Identify your opportunities

···→ Joys and sorrows of government income

···→ Examples of success

In the midst of a recession, when government-funding opportunities tanked for most nonprofits, a client snagged $100,000 in new government money. Government funds for nonprofits wax and wane. Yet as long as there are governments, nonprofit funding opportunities will exist. Historically, government funds constitute at least 21 percent of nonprofit income, making it the third-largest source for the sector in the United States. In Canada, it's 32 percent. Many, but not all, nonprofits can earn this income. Notable exceptions include faith-based groups that only proselytize and entities that promote controversial issues.

How Does Government Funding Work?

Government funding usually is offered to fund services to the community for the common good. Government distributes many resources through competitive grant processes, such as the following:

1. A government agency announces the availability of funds, the rules of the competition, the application required, and a submission deadline.

2. Nonprofits prepare materials and submit applications by the deadline.

3. Government staff reviews each submission and forwards completed applications to a review panel for evaluation. The panel, which consists of interested citizens and experts, scores the submissions using a prepublicized evaluation form.

4. Based on the score, the panel recommends the distribution of funds. Sometimes the panel makes the final decision. In other cases, the panel forwards recommendations to a governing body that makes the decision.

5. Recommended agencies receive a boilerplate contract.

6. After the contract is executed, the nonprofit delivers the services, provides proof they were delivered, and "bills" the government. When the paperwork is satisfactory, the nonprofit receives payment.

7. A year later, the nonprofit repeats this process by applying for new funds.

Government funds also are distributed through "earmarks," although these are less common than grant funding. Nonprofits obtain these earmarks by working with elected representatives. The official inserts an appropriation

---

Government Funding 101

Mission income, individual donations, and government funds represent the three largest nonprofit income streams. Most government funding is earned revenue obtained by offering services. Government funding involves extensive paperwork and other requirements, but the rewards can be great. Most awards exceed $10,000. Some exceed $1 million.

principle

for the nonprofit funding into a government document, such as a budget. If funded, the nonprofit obtains the income—again, after executing a contract.

Success with earmarks depends on your project's merit, your relationship with your representative, and a host of political events. Each representative has a particular earmark process. Jonathan Rauch, writing for *National Journal*, reports that one representative received one thousand earmark requests yearly from all sources, including nonprofits. The representative selected one hundred projects. About one in three were funded.

A final way that nonprofits obtain government revenue is through public-nonprofit partnerships. Partnerships are formed to solve complex community challenges, such as homelessness, helping youth reach their potential, and changing neighborhoods.

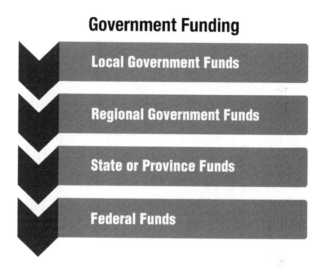

Government Funding

Local Government Funds

Regional Government Funds

State or Province Funds

Federal Funds

Income often begins after several years of planning (except in the case of disaster relief) and includes projects like charter schools or urban development efforts such as establishing land trusts.

Grants, earmarks, and partnerships represent the three main opportunities nonprofits have to obtain government funds. Next, you will learn about how to research government grant opportunities, the most common way to access this income.

Where Can You Find Government Funding?

To find government grants, identify government agencies whose missions complement your work. On the local, state, or provincial level, a quick way to do this is to visit the appropriate website and scan for departments of interests. Thus, an art gallery looks for agencies involved in tourist

---

To Apply or Not to Apply

In your search for government funds, you discover a fabulous opportunity. Unfortunately, the deadline is in two weeks. Is it a good idea to "drop everything" and apply?

Usually, no. First, you will have a very short period to compile the application. While this is common, your toughest competition will have anticipated the opportunity. With these kinds of headwinds, most nonprofits are better off focusing on less risky investments. Furthermore, since many government programs are cyclical, you can use your time to get a head start for the next round.

watch out!

---

development, education, and art. In the United States, on the federal level, the site to use for your research is grants.gov, the clearinghouse for federal opportunities. In Canada (the site is canada.ca), select a language (English or French) and enter "grants" in the site's search function.

As you search for opportunities, don't forget to look at quasi-government entities. Depending on your nonprofit's focus, you might include regional planning councils and water districts. These entities might offer grant programs that will fund your nonprofit.

If you are new to the government-funding arena, it helps to begin with local and regional opportunities. This will allow you to meet people, learn the process, and ask your peers for advice. Experience with local agencies will prepare your nonprofit for more remote sources. Most groups move from local to provincial or state opportunities and then to national offerings. When The Circus Arts Conservatory of Sarasota, Florida, started, it first won local county funding. The next year, it won state funds. Several years later, it received federal money.

After you list potential government partners, the next step is to understand any grant programs they offer. You want to know each program's goals and funding processes. Learn more by scanning website materials and other documents. Find a contact person to interview. Send questions by email. For opportunities where you have a strong interest, ask for a telephone interview to grow your understanding of the opportunity. Finally, after gathering the information, determine if the program fits your needs and decide if you will apply.

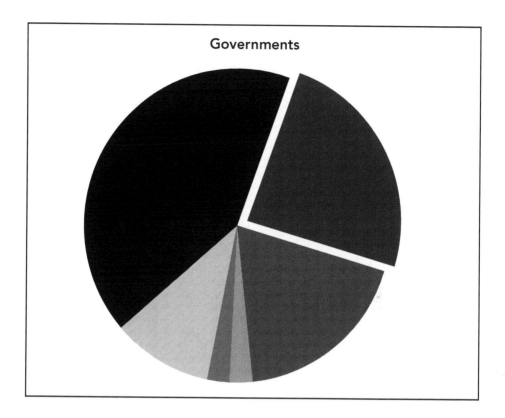

If you have multiple choices, prioritize technical assistance (TA) grants as a starting place. Most require relatively simple applications and offer extensive help. Maryland's Department of Housing and Community Development, for instance, has a technical assistance grant "to obtain or provide advisory, consultative, training, information, and other services which will assist or carry out community development activities." Most TA grants provide excellent small project funding. By participating, you will learn about the agency's processes, needs, and more about grant funding. Just as important, the opportunity will allow you to meet staff, officials, and leaders in your interest area. Technical assistance grants are a great way to test-drive a government agency's funding process.

Why Do Governments Provide Money to Nonprofits?

Now that you know where to hunt for government opportunities, you can increase your odds of success by understanding why these entities provide funds to nonprofits. What do they want to accomplish?

What motivates legislators to provide money to nonprofits? Each program, of course, has specific goals. In the big picture, the goals of government programs frequently fit into the following categories:

◆ Accomplishing a public good

◆ Securing voter approval

◆ Obtaining a better solution

◆ Obtaining bargains

For the Public Good

Government agencies, by nature, are designed to promote public good. Therefore, when government leaders find ways to accomplish this good by partnering with nonprofits, they have an incentive to invest. For example, hotel bed taxes in many communities support the arts. In return, the arts create economic, social, and other benefits. When hotel bed taxes are used to improve tourism, this in turns sells more hotel beds and supports greater economic strength.

Voter Approval

Because elected officials often make decisions with an eye to reelection, these funds are more available to nonprofits that voters view as doing essential work and for which there is broad agreement. Thus, animal shelters that handle dogs or cats that are public nuisances yield more funding. Nonprofits such as Planned Parenthood tend to be controversial and yield less funding.

**A Time for Everything—
Information Gathering**

If you seek information only, avoid contacting agencies during competitive funding cycles. This is the period between when they announce the availability of funds and the submittal deadline. To make the competition fair, most agencies observe strict guidelines about communications during these periods. I've called for information about programs for clients in the exploratory stage and was unable to convince the staff that I wanted *only* information—until after the deadline. After the deadline, you'll find staff much more informative.

practical tip

Better Solutions

When nonprofits offer the best-available solutions to community challenges, government investments provide great value. Nonprofits with great solutions provide the government with expertise, expanded resources, and improved results.

Grand Slam: Tapping All Seven Sources

The Early Learning Coalition of Florida's Heartland, Inc., is required to obtain a 6 percent local match to the millions of dollars in government funding it receives for low-income child care. At the same time, it must keep administrative expenses low, not lobby, and refrain from some traditional individual-fundraising activities. For instance, since the state governor appoints some board members, donations cannot be required. Nonetheless, the coalition developed a diverse funding base that taps all seven nonprofit income sources:

◆ It receives mission income from fees for classes it offers to child care providers.

◆ It participates in the local community foundation's online database to procure funds to sponsor children on the waiting list.

◆ It seeks funds from local foundations, United Ways, and corporations for the match, plus extras.

◆ In the unrelated-income category, money from the in-office snack bar provides funds for hospitality items, such as coffee for board meetings. (Government regulations often prohibit food purchases.)

◆ Donations of new and used books represent in-kind funding.

"Since we serve several rural counties, we can request match waivers for these areas," explains Executive Director Anne Bouhebent. "We see the benefits of earning the match. It increases community engagement and secures more resources for our children."

stories from the real world

Bargains

The last reason governments fund nonprofits is less discussed but is important to your investigation of potential nonprofit income sources. Nonprofit services can be bargains. For-profit solutions must provide profits. Nonprofit solutions do not. Since nonprofits often offer lower wages and fewer benefits, nonprofit costs are generally lower than for-profit costs and can be lower even than government costs.

What Are the Benefits of Government Funding?

So far, you have learned about government funding, its common forms, and where to hunt for opportunities. You also read about a handful of reasons why government agencies fund nonprofits. Now I return to your nonprofit. Will government funding fit your nonprofit's needs and culture? Why might *you* be interested in this income? From your nonprofit's viewpoint, here are four benefits:

Sizable Money

Obtaining government funding usually creates generous funding. The funds that nonprofits receive from grants, contracts, earmarks, and partnerships run from multiple thousands to multiple millions of dollars. While getting checks from government agencies takes time and effort, knowing that $100,000 will be deposited in your account before the end of the month offers great peace of mind.

The More the Merrier

One secret of successful government funding, according to Jack Humburg, director of housing development at the Boley Centers in Saint Petersburg, Florida, is to design your grant projects to be funded from multiple sources. As a builder and provider of housing for 1,200 special-needs individuals, Boley often puts together projects with several foundations and government entities. One recent apartment complex involved stacking six sources, including federal, state, and corporate income.

practical
tip

Rinse and Repeat—Often

Many government programs are available annually. The biggest challenge is developing and submitting the first proposal. Redoing the application for years two, three, and four takes time, but the rate of return per hour invested is much higher. The stability of many government opportunities is a boon to nonprofit budgets.

Credibility

Receiving funds from a prestigious foundation, government, or other entity can be like winning the Good Housekeeping Seal. It enhances credibility. For an unknown nonprofit, winning a competitive government grant can instantly provide cachet (distinction, prestige). Government funding can enhance your organization's brand. For example, when I travel, I review theater options. When multiple options exist, I gravitate to presenters funded by the National Endowment for the Arts as a sign of artistic quality.

Bland Necessities

As part of regular budgets, most nonprofits must "buy tires"—that is, items with low donor appeal. Since government work is fundamentally practical, government funds often "pay for tires." To maintain good transportation systems, governments pay for roads and traffic signs. Governments pay for twenty-four-hour police and fire protection. Therefore, government agencies understand the need for practical items, such as round-the-clock care for people with special needs.

Challenges

You just read about some very appealing benefits: big chunks of money, increased credibility, funds for unpopular items, and repeat funding. Yet every income source has its benefits and challenges. Government funding is no different. This section shares some of the challenges of government funding. Understanding these challenges helps you decide if government funds will work for your nonprofit.

Erroneous Perceptions

When other potential income partners—corporations, foundations, and individuals—learn you are government funded, they may judge that your

Another Way to Work with Government Agencies

Many nonprofits involved in government funding learn to add programs as funds become available, much like a train adds railway cars. The Community Based Care of Central Florida (CBC) experience illustrates "another way" to work with government agencies. CBC obtains government funds in bulk, with up to ten years of funding commitment to serve children in the child-welfare system. Along with the money, CBC accepts this responsibility: CBC must serve all who need services, with no waiting lists. If more children need services, CBC must raise funds to serve them. It can invest any extra funds to prevent children from entering the system.

With the funds, CBC buys services from other children's services providers. When these providers produce results, CBC can offer them greater financial stability, a voice in future investments, and rewards. Furthermore, long-term funding and control incentivizes CBC to serve children soon to minimize the expenses. If today a child needs $1,000 or even $10,000 in services that prevent greater costs later, CBC invests the funds.

The most important results is what it achieves in children's lives. For years, Florida ranked at the bottom in state-by-state comparisons of children served by foster care. Today, according to Right for Kids, the state ranks among the top-five providers. In the CBC service area, the number of foster children was reduced by 35 percent in less than ten years.

	Nonprofit	**Government**
Gains	"Unrestricted" money to fix problem	Known cost
Accepts	◆ Responsibility for solution ◆ Unknown downside risk	Lack of control over methods

stories from the real world

work is not their responsibility. They may erroneously believe their help is not needed because "the government takes care of it." You can educate those willing to learn that government funding is just one component of your sustainable income strategy.

Bureaucracy

When I ran Sarasota County's Community Development Block Grant program, the county provided funds for about a dozen projects, including those with several nonprofit entities. Mack Reid, the CEO of the Boys and Girls Club, was ready, willing, and cheerful about doing what was needed. Once, I called him at 3 p.m., apologizing and asking him to sign yet another piece of paper and have it notarized by 5 p.m. He took on the task. Not surprisingly, of all the projects, the club had its roof-replacement project completed first. His story offers two pieces of wisdom: First, to obtain the funds you must be responsive. Second, you will probably have to satisfy seemingly endless bureaucratic requirements.

Low Skill Transfer

Over time, the culture that major government funding creates can disrupt a nonprofit's efforts to make inroads into other income streams. The skills developed to win and administer government funds transfer poorly to other nonprofit revenue situations. Learning how to fill out the form to request a check does not grow your skills establishing a relationship with Mr. Donor. In contrast, working with Mrs. Bigbucks does help you develop better people skills to use with Mr. Donor.

Community Division

Government funding is inherently competitive, even when collaboration is required to obtain it. The stakes are high in this winner-takes-all process. Each application asks you to compare and contrast your services with others. In response, you write about your strengths and gently suggest that others provide inferior approaches. To succeed in solving complex human challenges, you must partner with others. Yet when the resources are scarce, leaving everyone money stressed, it's hard to play nice—even on paper. Competitive government funding can divide potential partners.

Addictive

Overall, the biggest challenge with government funding is the combination of two factors: large sums and weak control over future access. With government funds, you control your application and, if successful, your product. Most nonprofits exert minimal control over the political process that creates the opportunities. Repeatedly, nonprofit leaders who receive significant income from government agencies tell me of their commitment to rely less on it in the future. They invest energy and money to replace these funds. However, when attractive new government funding becomes available, most cease diversification efforts. Nonprofits sometimes act as if government funds are addictive.

Despite these and other challenges, many nonprofits find that government funds are worthwhile. Martha Macris, executive director of Memorial Assistance Ministries in Houston, put it this way: "As long as it is ethical, I believe it is our job to accept government money. It helps the clients. Besides, if you don't partner with the government, you relinquish your seat at the table."

To Recap

- ◆ Hundreds of government funding sources exist. Many provide significant income to nonprofits. Without this support, many vital services would suffer.

- ◆ Governments fund nonprofits to obtain public good, win voter approval, and foster better solutions—and also because they are bargains.

- ◆ Can your nonprofit earn government funding? Yes, for the vast majority of nonprofit organizations. Sources include local, state or provincial, federal, and quasi-government sources.

- ◆ Be wary of potential "addiction" to government funds and other challenges. Develop other sources of income, and create backup plans for fluctuations and possible disappearance.

Chapter Four

Stream Four—Foundations and Other Grantmaking Entities

IN THIS CHAPTER

- ···◆ Can you really spin words into gold?

- ···◆ Why do foundations and other grant entities donate money to nonprofits?

- ···◆ Three grant success keys: source, content, and relationship

- ···◆ Pluses and minuses of grant income

- ···◆ Examples of success

Approximately 125,000 foundations exist in the United States and Canada. A few are vast, such as Ford, Rockefeller, and Gates. They own recognizable names and tremendous assets. Most foundations are small. They share great similarities with individual donors. Foundation funding represents about 2 to 4 percent of nonprofit income, just a sliver of the income pie. Foundation funding, however, is far more important than the percentages indicate. Besides helping with capital projects and one-time equipment purchases, grants from foundations often fund nonprofit capacity building and new initiatives. For example, a foundation funds a new project to help The Wellness Community of Southwest Florida better serve Hispanic women.

Grants 101

Corporate funding, foundations, and unrelated income represent the three smaller sources of income for nonprofit organizations. Money awarded by foundations and other grant sources is considered donated funds. While hundreds of thousands of grant sources exist in North America, most nonprofits succeed with fifty or fewer sources. The majority of grants fall in the $5,000 to $100,000 range.

principle

Can You Really Spin Words into Gold?

Yes. You can write a one-page letter and obtain $5,000, $50,000, or even $500,000 with it. However, consistent success with grants requires a combination of tasks far more complex than simply crafting words well, uploading those words, and hitting the send button. Grants, like all other forms of nonprofit income, are about partnerships. It's true that some grant funders, including foundations, take a small risk and award funds to nonprofits they do not know, often because they love the grant idea, mission, or personnel behind it. Few invest significant money without knowing a lot about the organization receiving the investment.

Are foundations burdened by excess money that they have few opportunities to spend? While it would be fun if true, most foundations and other grant-giving entities face difficult choices about investing limited funds. They often receive few *quality* applications that meet their goals. The James Graham Brown Foundation in Louisville, Kentucky, began funding the Brown Fellows Program at Centre College and The University of Louisville. The impetus for the program was disappointment with funding requests from institutions of higher education, such as building and deferred maintenance. The foundation created the Brown Fellows Program. It awards full-ride-plus scholarships to twenty undergraduates a year, meeting the foundation's goal to promote the wellbeing of the citizens of Louisville and Kentucky. The colleges gain top students, tuition fees, and a closer relationship with the foundation.

To obtain foundation or other competitive grant funding, you must draft compelling funding requests that help the giving entity meet its goals. While each grant source has distinct guidelines and goals, most grant requests fall into one of three categories:

◆ *Capital requests.* Requests for building or durable goods with a life span of five or more years.

◆ *Program expansion.* For instance, funds for a limited time to provide an existing program in a new geographic area.

◆ *Solutions.* Funds that buy one-time solutions with long-term, positive cash-flow consequences, such as solar panels to dramatically reduce utility costs.

Grant-funding entities tend to avoid requests for:

◆ Operating expenses. People who give grants often shun supporting items that leave a nonprofit with the same need in twelve months, since these requests only move the problem forward 365 days.

◆ Salaries for founders when no salary has been paid to date, or similar items donated in the past. These funds buy few new community benefits.

Grant-Giving Entities

What are grant-giving entities? This chapter discusses a variety of organizations that provide grants to nonprofits. They include the following:

Private Foundations

Private foundations own a large body of funds that earn interest in the market. They provide a percentage of the value of assets back to qualified nonprofit organizations, often in the form of grants.

Community Foundations

Community foundations generally serve a community (e.g., Toronto) or a population subgroup (Lutherans). They collect funds from a variety of donors, earn management fees on the money, and oversee grant making to nonprofits based on the goals of the foundation and the individual donors.

Federated Funds

Federated funds, such as United Way, provide grants from funds they collect or earn. Examples include some Rotary Clubs, wine and food festivals, and neighborhood associations.

◆ Items that do not serve customers, such as your staff lounge, administrative office renovation, and the like.

Yes, you can spin words into gold. Similar to the "rights" associated with major gifts in an earlier chapter, spinning words into gold requires the right words, in the right circumstances, to the right party, for the right need.

Why Do Foundations and Other Grant Entities Donate Money to Nonprofits?

Foundations and other entities provide funding for many reasons. In part, it is a legal requirement. In the United States, private foundations must pay out an annual average of 5 percent of their assets.

A more mission-driven reason for giving to nonprofits is that this is how foundations and others meet their goals. These entities provide money to nonprofits because they (the givers) cannot do the work that is needed.

Follow the Plan and Reap the Rewards

Cindy, a manager at a food bank, directs a shipment of lettuce into the cooler. The worn and sagging produce boxes are too wide for the cooler door. The forklift must be abandoned. Each cardboard flat is hand carried inside.

The loud speaker clicks to call her to the telephone. After Cindy says hello, Jill introduces herself. She is from a foundation interested in making a gift. "What do you need?" she asks.

Cindy sees the cooler and the forklift. She resists the temptation to ask for a $20,000 fix. Instead, she follows her organization's plan. "Jill, thank you," Cindy replies. "The person to talk to is Kristen, our development director. Can I get your name and number so she can call you?"

Before contacting Jill, Kristen researches the foundation. In several months, the food bank receives a check for $150,000, more than seven times Cindy's quick-fix price. To increase your revenue, create or designate a key grant contact person, like Kristen.

 stories from the real world

---

Many foundations have specific requirements. Earlier, I mentioned the Brown Foundation's goal to promote the wellbeing of Louisville and Kentucky. In contrast, the DJ&T Foundation seeks to reduce pet overpopulation. The Lilly Endowment's goals concern community development, education, and religion.

Does it surprise you to learn that foundations often feel that their funds are miniscule compared with their needs? To achieve their goals, grant-giving entities like to see funds leveraged to maximize benefits. Successful nonprofits find ways to offer foundations and others like them "bargains." For instance, a foundation gives funds for a nonprofit to purchase a $30,000 truck. The truck allows the nonprofit to collect fresh food and provide $50,000 worth of food to the community's hungry every year for more than ten years. Thus, over time, the $30,000 truck provides $500,000 in value, an outstanding investment. Foundations seek meaningful changes in the community. By giving grants, they engage nonprofits to reach these goals.

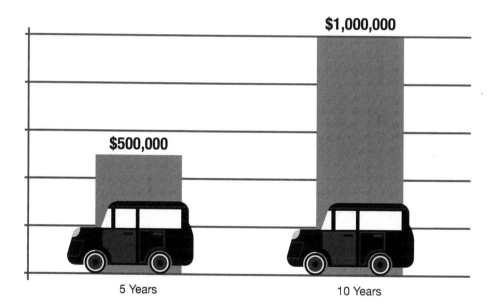

Three Grant Success Keys: Source, Content, and Relationship

You can't make a cake without sugar and eggs, nor can you succeed in obtaining grants from foundations and others without some key ingredients. These include the "right" who (source), what (content), and how (relationship).

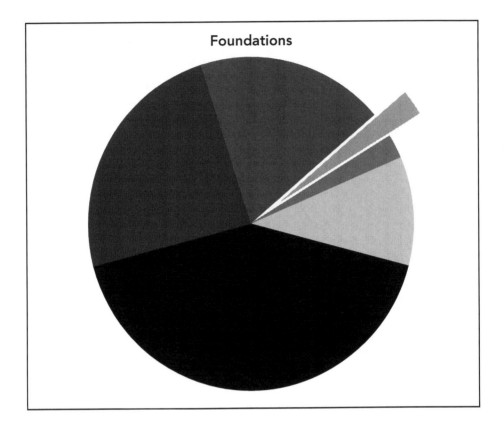

The Who (Source)

For your nonprofit to succeed in winning grant funding, you must identify foundations and other grant-giving entities with the propensity to fund nonprofit organizations like yours (the *who*). If a local foundation serves the military and your nonprofit has no relationship to the military, then your nonprofit fails this critical must. Look for these three pieces of evidence as indicators of a good match:

◆ You meet the guidelines as published on the website or elsewhere.

◆ The funder's grant-giving history indicates a strong interest in your cause. Many foundations list numerous interests and fund only a fraction of them.

◆ The foundation funds nonprofits in your geographic area, or it exhibits a pattern of national or international funding that involves your region. One of my clients, a locally focused organization, sought funding from a foundation that supports an end to euthanizing healthy pets. This foundation's recent history indicated a lack of regional funding, but strong national interest. My client applied and received funds.

The What (Content)

Once you identify a foundation or organization that fits your nonprofit, the next key is identifying *what* you will request. This includes an estimate of the dollars needed. Answer this question: "What, of all our needs and ideas, will help this grant funder meet its goals?" Answering this "right" is key to the success of your application. No matter how beautiful your eventual proposal or how appropriate your source, if you don't ask for something that appeals to the entity giving the grant, you will not succeed. In some cases, this is easy. A nonprofit obtains $15,000 in scholarships each year. Over the years, the nonprofit tries other amounts and requests. All are denied. So each year, the nonprofit refreshes the last application, tells a new success story, and hits send. In other cases, discerning what will interest a grant funder takes much more effort. For help, find answers to the following questions:

◆ What projects have they funded in three recent grant cycles?

◆ What needs would funding from the foundation solve, hopefully forever?

◆ What part of the foundation's mission can we help them meet?

The How (Relationship)

The *how* concerns your partnership with the grant provider. If you meet the guidelines, you can apply cold, without an existing relationship. In some cases, this is the only option. Ideally, however, staff members establish a healthy relationship with the grant-funding entity before drafting a proposal. The interaction gives the grant funder a sense of how your nonprofit conducts business and confidence that you will fulfill expectations and the promises made in a request. You can sometimes simply telephone a foundation representative and initiate a meeting. In other cases, meetings are impossible until after the application is submitted and only if the foundation requests a meeting.

> ### Think Like a Pilot
>
> "For new programs, use your initial grant funding to create a pilot," advises Susan Motley, the executive director of Medical Society of Virginia Foundation. "Then during the pilot, develop a business model to sustain or at least retain the best elements of the program."
>
>  practical tip

Prefer fragile relationships over none. Think about it this way. You need to leave one hundred dollars in cash for a friend to pick up. Do you choose an unknown person or a pesonal contact? Most people choose the personal contact.

Even though it is difficult for eager nonprofits to be patient, proceed slowly and methodically. Seek to know more about the needs of those giving the grants. Nonprofits that ask for money too soon receive rejections. Just as with individual donors, it may take months to develop a relationship, gain insight, and identify funding concepts of interest. The good news is that for many grant-funding entities, once you are "in," there is a good chance that your nonprofit can obtain future grants from the same source.

Pluses of Foundation Funding

At their best, grants provide nonprofits with venture capital. They change lives now and reach into the future. Foundation or grant funding has helped create public libraries, the 911 emergency system, Sesame Street, and white lines on the highways. Besides progressive community improvements, nonprofits obtain other benefits from grants.

Big Checks

Funding from major foundations and other grant sources is generally large. When your average membership income provides fifty dollars a head, a grant of $25,000 thrills.

Partnership

Grant-giving organizations and nonprofits enjoy a special partnership. Why? Compared with other nonprofit income sources, these groups share great affinity. The goals of each closely align in areas such as creating change, improving communities, and quality-of-life issues. A foundation that specializes in strengthening senior care is interested in your nonprofit as you implement new ideas to support caretakers. Even if a foundation fails to fund you immediately, it is likely that your mutual work will continue to bring you together. The foundation might provide other

---

Is Your Nonprofit Ready to Apply for a Grant?

It might be if these criteria are satisfied:

◆ Your organization meets certain minimum qualifications, e.g., it has an IRS letter conferring 501(c)(3) status.

◆ Your organization enlists the support of a credible board of directors, such as five or more community members (besides relatives and close friends) who care about the cause and can give or help you obtain resources.

◆ You've identified a service that will help your community.

◆ Your service does not duplicate another organization's efforts in the same location, especially one with a well-established track record.

◆ Your organization's history suggests the approach you propose will succeed.

◆ You have a plan for how the program will continue after the grant funds are spent.

◆ You have a specific purpose for your request, and it's consistent with funder goals.

◆ You have realistic expectations about the amount, kind, and timing of your grant requests.

Example

kinds of help, such as keeping senior concerns in the headlines, valuable contacts, and perhaps encouragement.

Besides partnerships with the foundation, many grants require partnerships with other nonprofits. While many of these working relationships don't last beyond the grant, the arrangement can provide new resources and ideas to your nonprofit.

Prestige

In the credits for documentaries, you have undoubtedly seen the names of prestigious foundations. Funding from a foundation and similar groups provides your nonprofit an opportunity to improve its branding. You can leverage the foundation's public prestige by issuing a press release to announce funding and by carrying the information on your website.

Complements Individual Fundraising

Another benefit of grant funding is that it can be designed to complement your nonprofit's individual fundraising efforts. For instance, most grant applications request information on additional income sources. They increasingly require information on board giving. If you have a reluctant board, grant funds might prove to be the incentive your board members need to participate. Another option is using potential foundation grants to inspire individual gifts by asking the foundation to grant your funds as a challenge grant.

Good Discipline

While difficult to appreciate in the midst of application preparations, grants help nonprofits stay healthy. Grant applications force extremely busy nonprofits to plan. How so? Many applications ask nonprofits to have specific plans and to clarify thinking. Without the motivation of funding, many nonprofits would abandon good planning to respond to urgent needs.

Completing a grant application can be like your dental hygienist asking if you flossed. You know the right answer is affirmative. This grant discipline includes completing audits, doing marketing, stating board-giving rates, making succession plans, etc. Do you have a strategic plan? The correct answer, just like with flossing, is yes. Without grants, many housekeeping items would get lost in the whirlwind of daily life.

Income provided by foundations and other grant-giving entities provides significant benefits, including income. Grants induce nonprofits to step back, think ahead, form partnerships, improve brands, take action, and even enhance individual fundraising.

Challenges of Foundation Funding

Foundation and other grant-related funding has its own unique challenges (not to be confused with "challenge grants"). Funding from foundations and other grant-giving entities challenges nonprofits because:

It's the Foundation's Mission, Not Yours

Upon announcement of an estimated $200 million estate gift to The Patterson Foundation, every local nonprofit leader dreamed of winning large grants from the new funds. Later, when the foundation published its strategic initiatives, few of those dreams were fulfilled. The foundation came out with very specific guidelines. Foundations and other grant-giving entities fund grants that meet their interests. A challenge with this income source is that nonprofits must bend their needs into opportunities that help both entities reach separate goals. You can live in a community blessed with multiple foundations, but if your goals don't match, then those foundations will not provide income to your nonprofit. Funding from the Bill & Melinda Gates Foundation is frequently mentioned but infrequently obtained.

It's Never Enough

I alluded to this second challenge earlier. While foundations may have a lot of money, they seldom have amounts large enough to address the serious challenges they seek to solve. When leveraged and thoughtfully used, grant funds create great impacts. In contrast, potential gifts from individual donors are

---

Challenge Grant

A grant made with the condition that your nonprofit must raise, by a deadline, a certain amount of dollars from other sources. For instance, The Selby Foundation offers to give your organization a $50,000 grant for your capital campaign *only if* you raise the rest of the money needed for the campaign.

much larger. For the challenges they want to conquer, foundations, like nonprofits, are underfunded.

Short Hours

A final challenge with this income stream concerns limited access. Your nonprofit will only occasionally be able to tap income from foundations and other grant-giving entities. While each grant giver develops its own process, most streams such as United Way funding cannot be sought more than once per year. A supermarket charity restricts applications to once per year. A local foundation may allow you to apply only every third year. You will not be able to tap these funds as often as you'd like. Generally, grants from foundations and other grant-giving entities only supplement your other income streams.

While grants can do wonderful things for nonprofits, they cannot do everything. Nonetheless, most nonprofits seek and receive grants, enjoying the income and the opportunities they provide.

To Recap

◆ Grant income is possible for most nonprofits; however, grant funds are frequently not large enough, not always a good fit, and/or not dependable enough to provide consistent operating funds.

◆ Knowing who to ask, what to ask for, and creating a partnership with the grant funder are three important success factors in winning grants.

◆ Some needs are more grant appropriate than others. Grant makers prefer capital requests, funding expansions, and one-time activities that provide long-term gains.

◆ Besides money, grants help nonprofits step back, think ahead, form partnerships, improve brands, take action, and even enhance individual fundraising.

Chapter Five

Stream Five—Businesses Supporting Nonprofits

IN THIS CHAPTER

- ····→ Why do businesses provide nonprofits money?

- ····→ About business and corporate opportunities

- ····→ Why beg when you can partner?

- ····→ Pluses and minuses of for-profit income

- ····→ Examples of success

When the Tampa Bay History Center designed its $52.5 million building, it wanted to offer guests great food services but didn't want to become a food vendor. Instead, it partnered with Columbia, Florida's oldest restaurant. The Tampa Bay History Center receives a percentage of the eatery's proceeds and rental fees for the space. "Inside the center," explains C. J. Roberts, the center's CEO, "visitors learn about Cuban sandwiches. On the way out, they can eat one."

Business support for nonprofits comes from grants, sponsorships, cause marketing, and contractual relationships, such as the one enjoyed by the Tampa Bay History Center. Nonprofit business income achieves two goals: nonprofit support and enhanced business outcomes. In the grand scheme of nonprofit income, business funding is miniscule. However, since nonprofit funding from this source exceeds $1.5 trillion a year, even the 1 to 2 percent it represents is an important source for many nonprofits.

Nonprofit partnerships with businesses are in their infancy and hold huge potential. Both sectors share a desire to reach key markets with messages. Both are in the early stages of learning to work together and often "do it poorly," according to Brent Barootes, president of the Partnership Group in Canada. Nonprofits are beginning to tap into budget line items, such as human resources and marketing. These budgets are usually much bigger than those for philanthropy. The best nonprofit arrangements with corporate partners are still being developed. Your nonprofit might develop a new breakthrough idea to earn corporate income.

What Is Corporate Funding?

Corporate funding is money that originates from a business. It may take the form of a fifty dollar gift, the purchase of a $2,000 special-event table, or a long-term arrangement that provides a nonprofit hundreds of thousands of dollars. This section discusses several common corporate opportunities.

Donated Funds

Your nonprofit may receive grants or a donation from a business or an associated entity such as the GE Foundation. Corporate gift and distribution processes vary. Some businesses pick one or a small number of nonprofits to support. Other corporations offer competitive grant opportunities. Matching gifts connected to a current corporate employee or a retiree are another possibility.

Earned: From an Ad to the Moon

Earned income represents a second opportunity to obtain income from corporations. The most famous example of earned income is the relationship between the Statue of Liberty Foundation and American Express. This cause marketing promotion raised $1.7 million for Lady Liberty and nearby Ellis Island. To access potential business income, you will need to help the business achieve its goals. The Tampa Bay History Center helped the Columbia Restaurant Group profit from selling food on site and from advertising the other Columbia restaurants. While the business may use funds from its community goodwill budget to pay you, earned income often taps into marketing, human resources, or other budget lines.

Here are three distinct ways nonprofits earn money from for-profits:

◆ *Advertising.* The back pages of your program contain a collection of business cards and other ads inviting patrons to use its services. Selling advertisements is a very common source of corporate income. In this case, you sell ads in your print and online publications that provide businesses with exposure to potential customers and enhanced branding by demonstrating community involvement.

◆ *Cause marketing.* Cause marketing is where a business promotes both its product or service and the nonprofit, such as the American Express promotion. Other examples include affinity credit cards and special days when a percentage of sales go to a nonprofit. In cause marketing, nonprofit income increases as the company's sales increase. To clarify everyone's expectations, both parties establish in advance certain campaign limits, such as dates and maximum dollar amounts.

◆ *Sponsorships.* People familiar with the sponsorship concept immediately think of special events. Here a business receives special recognition at the event in return for a contribution. However, sponsorships can be much broader. Well-developed sponsorships involve packages that include advertising, cause marketing, events, a donation, and ways to experience the business's service or product. They can involve the nonprofit accessing multiple business budget lines. (Note: In the United States, according to the IRS, "advertising" received as a result of sponsorship negates the deductibility of any charitable contribution—so make sure your business partners check with their accountants.)

Brent Barootes, president of the Partnership Group, a Canadian consulting firm that specializes in sponsorships, draws a distinction between advertising and sponsorship. In his *Tuesday Morning Commentary* newsletter, he writes:

Advertising is a medium that pushes out messaging. Whether on a billboard, TV, Facebook, radio, or print, it is one dimensional.... Sponsorship is experiential. It mixes emotion with an offer or message.

Ideally, sponsorship provides a win for the audience, the nonprofit, and the business. For instance, in a five-kilometer race, a corporate sponsor provides runners free samples of its sports drink. The sponsor provides volunteers to help on race day, contributes to the prize, and receives public recognition. After the race, runners receive discount coupons for the drink in the nonprofit's follow-up mailing.

Like all other sources of income, working with corporations to obtain funds involves helping both the nonprofit and the business obtain value. Of all the seven nonprofit funding streams, business funding demands thinking about this value exchange upfront and with great clarity.

Corporate Funding 101

Corporate funding, foundations, and unrelated income represent the three smaller sources of nonprofit income. Business funding can be donated, earned—or, intriguingly, both.

Throughout this chapter, I use the words *corporation, company, firm, for-profit,* and *business* interchangeably. This is to encourage you to consider different kinds of for-profit entities, from small stores to service organizations, sports teams, conglomerates, utility companies, and every entity in between, as potential partners. For more information on corporate giving, read Linda Lysakowski's *Raise More Money from Your Business Community,* published by CharityChannel Press.

 practical tip

Why Do Corporations Give Nonprofits Money?

Imagine yourself in the shoes of a business owner. It's year-end. Your business plans to make a donation. You have an array of opportunities on your desk. A small committee selected two opportunities with great appeal. All else is equal, except one opportunity also will help you achieve your business goals next year. Naturally, you select this one.

What value does a corporation seek when it provides income to your nonprofit? A business provides income to improve its own income. The businesses also provide money to increase customer loyalty, improve brands, engage employees, and improve the community—as well as because the business leader has an emotional connection to the nonprofit and/or cause. This section examines these motivations.

Increase Customer Loyalty

Smack in the middle of your Pendleton Woolen Mills clothing catalog is information about how a portion of the proceeds from your purchase of an American Indian College Fund Blanket helps tribal colleges. As you drive to work, you pass a nonprofit truck with an array of corporate logos, including your bank's. You are glad the hungry are fed and that your bank helps. Increasing customer loyalty is one common goal of nonprofit support. A recent *Wall Street Journal* article stated, "Research suggests that consumers are more likely to support companies that say they are making a difference in the world." In short, nonprofits receive money from businesses because these value exchanges support customer loyalty, resulting in increased profit.

> ### It Is Who They Know
>
> To support their favorite nonprofit, a group of supporters met with the owner of their favorite jewelry store. They invited him to help with their goal to build several Habitat for Humanity houses. Together they developed a sponsorship package that included a $5,000 store gift certificate for use in a raffle. They purchased the certificate for half price. "The store," Mike Mansfield, chief executive officer of the Charlotte County Habitat for Humanity said, "created the sponsorship package because the owner knew the group members. They were his customers, and the package was going to provide value to the store."

Branding

A hiking shoe manufacturer wants to distinguish itself from other brands. The friends-of-the-park group learns this and approaches the shoemaker with the concept of naming different shoes after different parks. The relationship helps this shoe manufacturer differentiate its shoes from the others. The shoes become the ones to wear in the parks. In the case of branding, the long-term outcome may be to increase sales, but funding the nonprofit is a tool used to establish market position.

Employee Loyalty and Pride

When the cashier checking out a nonprofit employee saw his lapel pin, she told him, "We love supporting the work you do with babies." While the categories so far have focused on external results, this benefit is internal. Businesses want to find top-flight employees and, once they find them, keep them. Supporting nonprofits is an opportunity for employees to "feel good" about employers.

Besides increasing loyalty and pride, businesses benefit when employees are active in the community. Most nonprofits are familiar with the employee of a bank, accounting firm or similar company who serves on the board, in part, to meet community members and, indirectly, to promote the firm. Businesses benefit when employees gain local information, relationships, skills, and a chance to be refreshed. Naturally, businesses prefer supporting nonprofits where its employees are active.

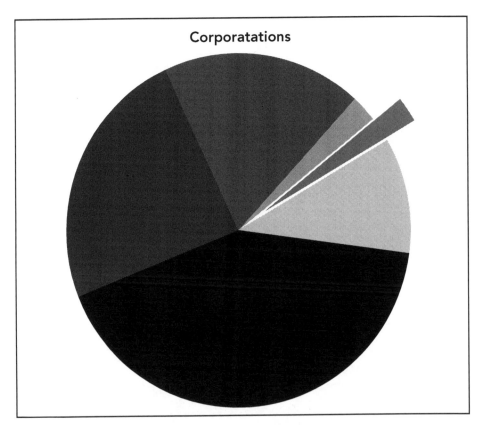

Better Communities

Thoughtful business leaders recognize that nonprofits improve the communities where they live and work. In turn, these improvements contribute to the business's long-term prospects. Therefore, supporting nonprofits makes long-term investment sense.

Individual Passions

Fred, a graduate of Hendrix College in Conway, Arkansas, loves his alma mater. Every year, Fred's business gives a substantial gift to Hendrix. Some business leaders use business resources to promote personal interests and passions. In essence, Fred's gift is an individual donation routed through the corporation. This mode of giving is mentioned here because it comes through corporations, and it is helpful to remember that something like an alumni connection may be the reason behind a gift.

Creating Relationships that Work

Envision organizing the contents of collection barrels, sacks of rice big enough for three adults to stand inside, and a mishmash of donated groceries. Houston Food Bank recruits volunteer help to organize and prepare food for distribution to 137,000 people each week. In a recent year, the food bank had over 23,500 individuals volunteer two hundred thousand hours!

How does the food bank obtain this help? First, it's open twenty-two hours a day. Second, it developed infrastructure that supports a first-rate experience for volunteers, including state-of-the-art sorting equipment. The distribution center also houses a conference center available at cost to businesses and community groups that often volunteer while on site.

For nonprofits that seek corporate donations, one of the most interesting aspects of the food bank operation is how it creates funding relationships as a natural byproduct of other activities. Corporate executives reviewing grant applications often already know a lot about the food bank's work because they've used the conference center.

stories from the real world

What Are The Benefits of Corporate Funding?

Money, of course, is the number-one benefit of developing relationships with for-profits. However, developing corporate partners can provide other benefits. We've listed several here to jump-start your thinking.

Mutual Promotion

Nonprofits and for-profits share a common goal. Both entities need people and seek to reach the right people effectively and efficiently. Businesses seek new customers and employees. Nonprofits seek new volunteers, customers, supporters, and donors. Both want to retain their current people. By working with a business to reach people, your nonprofit can greatly expand its reach.

Relative to most nonprofits, businesses have large budgets and a huge reach. Inclusion in a business's communications can result in more people hearing about your nonprofit's work. For example, some utilities allow nonprofit inserts in their monthly utility bill mailings. Here the nonprofit can advertise its services and request donations.

Professional Approach

Working with for-profits demands that nonprofits enter the world of business partners and, often, that they work with greater professionalism. Business culture is different, and it is important to recognize the differences. It demands shorter meetings. It means recognizing that consensus is not the only decision-making mode available. Businesses are often comfortable letting the boss decide. Over time, these and similar cultural differences might help you improve your current processes, better manage your time, and meet the expectations of different people. In short, embracing some aspects of the business culture will make you more competitive.

Love 'Em or Skip 'Em

Do business with businesses and businesspeople you like. Some businesses are more social minded; others are not. Your organization offers these businesses great value. To start, seek out the social-minded business that you like.

 practical tip

Other Help

Besides marketing and increased professionalism, businesses often provide "extras" to nonprofit partners. Assistance examples include referrals and vendor discounts. A business can ask its vendors to give you a price break. Others include suggesting board members, volunteers, and community contacts. Few mayors, for instance, can resist a request from a major employer to meet with a nonprofit leader over lunch. Likewise, businesses can help you access resources. If a project requires a professionally designed flyer, a company's design staff might create it—a resource you may lack.

Challenges

The evening his older brother left for college, my younger son gloried in eating all the leftovers at the evening meal. As our plates emptied, I reminded him that now that his brother was away, it would be his responsibility to do the dishes every night. "So," I asked, "how do you like being an only child?"

Can You Leverage Government and Foundation Income to Obtain Corporate Funding?

Yes, if you follow the approach used by Capital Workforce Partners in Hartford, Connecticut. It leverages corporate funding to serve more than five hundred youth interns each summer. How do they do it? First, Capital developed a multiyear internship program involving life skills, nonprofits, and corporate internships, according to Pam Nabors, formerly program operations director and currently president of Workforce Central Florida in Orlando, Florida. They fund this program with foundation, federal, state, and city sources. Then, to serve even more urban youth, Capital approaches corporations and asks them to sponsor youth interns for a fee ($1,000 to $1,600). Using its connections, Capital leverages any corporate investment into $7,000 or more in services. Some sponsoring corporations offer on-site internships. All participate in the celebrations and share information about how the firm supports the program with constituencies.

stories from the real world

"It's a mixed blessing," he muttered. For nonprofits, business income can also be a mixed blessing. This section explores some of the drawbacks of this income source.

Minimal Goal Overlap

Businesses are not in business to give money away to good causes. Nor are nonprofits in business to help businesses make sales. At best, the nonprofit and business relationship has minimal overlap, as illustrated. Nonprofits succeed in obtaining income from for-profits when they find ways to link nonprofit needs to business outcomes. If, for instance, a major employer has challenges finding trained employees and your nonprofit can provide them, you have an opportunity to create income.

Small Amounts

Most corporate donations are small. A few are multi-million-dollar exchanges. Donations of $1,000, $5,000, or $10,000 are common. Sometimes this is because corporate giving budgets are small. Other times, small donations can represent an intentional corporate strategy to maximize the publicity that gifts receive. One national grocery chain's foundation includes a list of over twenty pages of nonprofits it supports with many small gifts.

Value Estimates

Another challenge, especially with sponsorships, is setting a dollar amount on the value your nonprofit provides. For many nonprofits, this is new territory. Some nonprofits may be surprised to learn they have assets with value, even substantial value. For instance, several years ago, the Habitat for Humanity brand was valued at $3.1 billion. What value does your mailing list hold for a potential business partner? What value is it to be listed as a business partner on your sign that a quarter of a million cars pass every day? Does this value change if you add two business names? To offer value to potential business partners, you must make an inventory of your assets and calculate their values. These and similar value decisions must be made so that you can offer enticing and fair value to your nonprofit and to your business partners.

Staffing Challenges

You work with the director of marketing over several months developing a sponsorship agreement for a children's event. Just as you are about to sign the agreement, the firm is sold. Another challenge you will encounter with business income is that many issues impacting your relationships are beyond your control. Not only will you experience ownership changes, but you will encounter changes in the fiscal health of the firm and the economy, as well. Business partnerships can exist for years and provide stable income. Others can be tenuous from day one.

To Recap

◆ Corporate funding is a smaller slice of the nonprofit income pie, and it often takes the form of grants, advertisements, cause marketing, and sponsorships.

◆ Nonprofits build relationships with corporations to help both achieve goals.

◆ Businesses provide money to nonprofits to increase customer loyalty, improve branding, create employee pride, and improve the community where they do business.

◆ Business income challenges include small gift amounts, difficulty finding common ground, changes in staff and business environment, and uncertainties over how a nonprofit should value assets.

Chapter Six

Stream Six—Unrelated Income Opportunities

IN THIS CHAPTER

···→ Can you earn a profit?

···→ Possibilities limited only by imagination and resources

···→ Identify your opportunities

···→ Examples of success

"The income from the ReStores pays for our overhead," Renee Snyder, executive director of a Habitat for Humanity affiliate, announced. "Now every donated dollar we receive is used to build houses." Many Habitat affiliates earn income from ReStores. These stores sell surplus and reusable building supplies. The ReStore idea fits well with Habitat's mission and skills, and it provides significant income.

ReStores' earnings represent unrelated income, the sixth stream of nonprofit income. Unrelated income is a catchall category that involves no relationship to your mission. It represents 10 to 16 percent of all nonprofit income. Examples include food sales, endowment interest, and the money you made selling your used van. Most nonprofits earn some unrelated income. For some nonprofits, it provides substantial income.

Fourth Largest Source of Income

What is unrelated income? It is revenue that your nonprofit earns from providing a service or selling goods, where the product or service has little or no relationship to your mission. Unrelated income is the last of the small players in the nonprofit income game. Yet, while small for the sector as a whole, its size exceeds foundation and corporation income combined. It is the fourth-largest source of nonprofit income. Nonprofits sometimes dismiss unrelated income, thinking it equates to bake sales, car washes, and the like. As the examples show, it can be much more.

principle

Possibilities: Limited Only By Imagination, Resources, and Energy

How might your nonprofit earn unrelated income? Begin with a decision to seek it. Then decide if you will earn it by selling goods or services, if you will sell to retail or wholesale customers, and what else besides earning money you will accomplish through unrelated-income activities.

Decision: Goods or Services

Generally, to earn unrelated income, you sell services, such as some of your expertise, or you sell goods, like T-shirts or ice cream. Goods may be new or used. Consignment and used-goods stores are common. The latter, when done right, are "cash cows," according to Linda Osmundson, CEO at the nonprofit organization CASA (Community Action Stops Abuse) in Saint Petersburg, Florida, whose nonprofit earns significant funding this way.

Decision: Wholesale or Retail

You will also need to decide who your customers will be. Perhaps you own

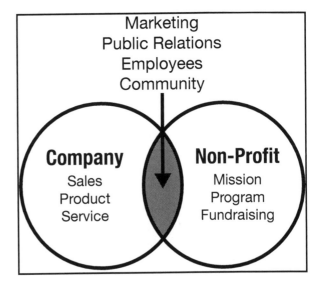

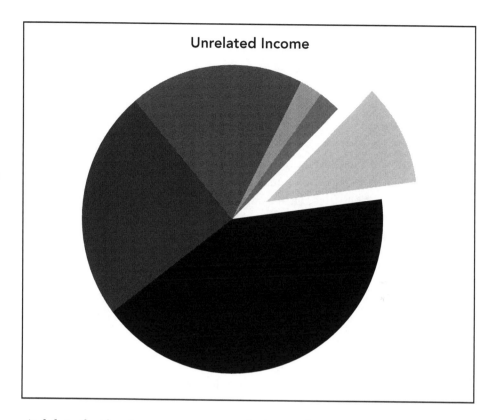

Unrelated Income

vital data that business customers seek. Or you have a process that other nonprofits can use to increase effectiveness. You might create items to sell to museum stores. You may sell services or goods to wholesale customers. These might include governments, corporations, foundations, and other nonprofits. Or, you may provide resources, such as snacks, directly to customers. Perhaps you provide a service that your customers would love, such as a tournament with the latest trading cards.

Decision: What Besides Income Do You Seek to Accomplish, if Anything?

Another set of decisions concerns the reasons you want to sell items or services. You may wish simply to earn income. You might also plan to accomplish other goals, such as enhance customer visits or please current customers. The Morikami Museum and Japanese Gardens, for instance, sells Japanese exports because customers always ask for help procuring them. The possibilities of what you might accomplish, besides earning money, are broad.

How Can You Identify Unrelated Income Sources?

If you decide to increase unrelated income at your nonprofit, where might you find opportunities? Below are "treasure spots" to look for unrelated-income opportunities.

Take Inventory

One way to grow unrelated income is to expand your current offerings. If you have a profitable beverage machine at one site, can you add another? If you rent your building once per quarter, can you rent it monthly? If your thrift store on the north side of town is going gangbusters, add a new one. Just like writers who create sequels to bestsellers, build on your current successes. List your existing income sources. Then explore opportunities to expand them.

Take a Fresh Look at Assets

Do you hold or own items, space, or even staff that is well loved, useful, and underutilized? If your part-time financial whiz seeks more hours, can

---

Unrelated Income 101

Good Wheels, in Fort Myers, Florida, provides transportation services for the disabled, including life-sustaining trips, such as those for medical appointments and senior dining. Almost three-quarters of its $10 million budget involves government funding. To fund the remaining 25 percent of the budget, Good Wheels developed three unrelated-income sources. Each source is based on Good Wheels' polished skills and agency knowhow.

The first is a charter bus company. It began by leasing three buses for five years. The fleet now averages forty vehicles. Second, Good Wheels sells advertising wraps on all its vehicles. Buyers pay for the wraps and a monthly fee of $750 to $1,000. Finally, to close the gap, Good Wheels provides vehicle maintenance based on its existing vehicle maintenance expertise. Customers include other nonprofits and individuals. Together, these three sources provide $300,000 in annual income.

stories from the real world

you provide her services to others for a fee? Is your space convenient to everything and vacant part of the day or week? A nonprofit that provided afterschool services earned income by renting space to a charter school during the school day. List your underutilized assets. Remember your special skills. For instance, if you serve children, you might be in an ideal situation to sell high-quality educational toys to their parents for holiday presents. After you identify underused assets, explore ways to use them to help you earn income.

Service Requests

Your customers are another source of ideas. Ask your team to record customer requests. Also note any errands customers mention needing someone to do. While these lists will provide more ideas, most of them will need to be adapted to work for you. You will not open a bank, but you might install a cash machine, such as the one that recently appeared at my farmer's market. Add to your list requests from people who are not local nonprofit customers. Do people ask for teen or family services? Do they wish someone like Sue would plan their next event? Listen. Collect ideas. People will tell you their needs. Some will provide income possibilities.

Artshound.com

Don't know what to do on a Saturday night? If you're in Houston, The Houston Arts Alliance can help. Use the alliance's calendar Artshound to decide. On a recent Saturday, it listed over 170 area events organized by venue, location, and start time.

The Houston Arts Alliance decided to help others develop online calendars. "Most calendars are not very good," explained Jonathan Glus, the alliance's CEO. "We knew, with our help, that other organizations could develop great ones." The impetus to provide the calendar service was inadequate income. The Houston Arts Alliance recognized an opportunity and invested in it. Now the alliance is well on its way to meeting a goal to raise $250,000 annually with the service. Customers include the University of Houston and local businesses.

stories from the real world

Innovate

When Henry Ford created Model Ts, he invented little. Instead, he combined existing manufacturing ideas in fresh ways. To find other ideas at your nonprofit, innovate. Combine existing ideas from the field or anywhere in new ways. For instance, a nonprofit adapts the concept of credit cards to collect customer data. Instead of signing in, customers swipe in. This speeds the process, improves data accuracy, and eases reporting. Once the nonprofit has the process working smoothly, it sells the process to other nonprofits to create unrelated income.

Before you select specific unrelated income opportunities to pursue, cast a wide net. Identify ten or even twenty possibilities. Then choose the best from them. Identify even fewer to pilot. The creative process is messy. If midway through you feel you have too many possibilities, then you are doing it right.

The Positive Side of Unrelated Income

Unrelated income, when unexpected, can be like finding a roll of twenties in your pants pocket. Unrelated income allows you to buy necessary items without obligation to others. Here are the top reasons your organization will want to explore unrelated income:

Do It and Done

When you earn unrelated income, you do not need to create mission outcomes. The goal is to make money. Customers anticipate only good customer experiences. They do not expect relationships

And Now for Something Completely Different . . .

Nonprofits normally strategize about how to inspire foundations to give them grants. Instead, have you ever considered providing fee-based services to a foundation? Family Services of Greater Houston did. A foundation with $10 million in assets contracted with Family Services to administer its grants for local nonprofits and nursing scholarships. How can you use this idea? Use it as a springboard to consider unusual ideas to grow your income. What is something *completely different* for you?

stories from the real world

or an emotional connection with your nonprofit. Even if you add these customers to your mailing list (a worthwhile idea to test), the relationship is strictly one of business.

Customer Convenience

Internally, you may have to treat unrelated income differently to comply with tax authorities. However, from your customer's viewpoint, the difference is immaterial. To learn more about a museum exhibit Amy just visited, she bought a book in the museum gift store about frogs (mission revenue) and chocolate cookies (unrelated income) to tide her over before dinner.

When done well, unrelated income items or services enhance customer experiences and solve needs. Why is this a benefit? Understanding that customers have multiple reasons to make purchases invites you to think

---

How MOSI Created Unrelated Income

MOSI, or the Museum of Science and Industry, is the fifth-largest science center in the United States. To solve a budget crisis several years ago, MOSI gathered a team of staff members and volunteers to conduct "a world cafe." Participants created ten potential money-generating activities to reduce the $400,000 shortfall. Four succeeded. The most successful was built around Yu-Gi-Oh! trading cards.

Through a press release, MOSI marketed the first Yu-Gi-Oh! tournament. It took place on a Sunday morning when MOSI is not busy. The first day, MOSI admitted four hundred guests at ten dollars each. Over the next months, MOSI rode the Yu-Gi-Oh! craze by hosting twice-monthly events.

MOSI's idea can be replicated. Youth-serving nonprofits across North America might host similar tournaments based on popular items. While you don't know yet what items will be popular, you do know that children are enamored with relatively low-cost collectibles like Beanie Babies or animal rubber bands. Can you create unrelated income like MOSI did?

stories from the real world

differently about unrelated income possibilities.

Potential for Significant Income

While many nonprofits earn incidental sums of unrelated income, such as bank interest and beverage machine proceeds, unrelated income need not be miniscule. Unrelated income might fund a major service or everything. For instance, the Boys and Girls Clubs of Manatee, Florida, received a golf course in a bequest, and the profits provide operating funds for one its clubs. Some nonprofits create

Interesting to Know

Funds given to create an endowment are a form of individual giving. To earn interest, you lend the money to another entity, such as a government treasury or a corporation. In return, the borrower pays you interest. Most endowment funds start with individual gifts. Later, the income earned is unrelated income.

More Than a Summer Love

The Chautauqua Institution lies on a lovely lake of the same name in New York State. Founded in 1874, it provides a nine-week, in-depth education program with over 2,200 events. Much like a college or university, 80 percent of its income comes from earned revenue. One of the institution's assets is the Athenaeum, a 156-room wooden hotel constructed in 1881.

Envision the challenges of owning a large hotel open only in the summer that requires year-round upkeep. To use this facility more and to serve new people, the institution expanded the hotel's season to the spring and fall. This extended season creates numerous income opportunities, such as weddings and Road Scholar programs, created by Elderhostel, the not-for-profit world leader in lifelong learning since 1975. The extended season also allows the kitchen to offer better employment and retain greater skills that support more of the institution's other food venues. With careful planning, Chautauqua turned a fiscal challenge into an asset that brings the Chautauqua experience to new people and provides more income.

parallel businesses to generate ongoing revenue. Most nonprofits dream of developing an endowment fund to offset operation costs. Unrelated income need not be chump change.

An Opportunity for Mission

A hospice provides its community meeting room to outside groups with one condition. A hospice representative will have an opportunity to welcome the group and briefly share its work. Unrelated income can be an opportunity to offer similar "mission moments" to new audiences. While such opportunities do not move the needle in your public recognition, they do bring your name to new people.

Unrelated Income Challenges

While unrelated income offers attractive benefits, it also brings challenges. Keeping in mind both benefits and challenges, consider how you might ameliorate your challenges by using the suggestions below.

A Sideshow

Unrelated income, by nature, is a secondary consideration. If not handled carefully, successes can distract stakeholders from other critical activities. To keep pursuit of unrelated income from overwhelming you, create an

---

What Kind of Income Does Your Special Event Create?

Is income from your gala unrelated income or individual giving? Most people firmly place galas in the category of individual giving. Is this correct? A friend attends the film festival's opening-night party because it "offers the best parties in town." Otherwise, she has only a passing interest in film. An orchestra holds an annual New Year's Eve ball. Attendees love celebrating the new year together. However, when the orchestra's leaders study event outcomes, they see that it generates little income, doesn't create new donors or reach prospects, and requires a huge time investment. After studying the facts, the orchestra cancels the gala. Investigate your events. Do they represent individual fundraising or unrelated income? Do the results justify the investment?

food for thought

advisory team to supervise. Set limits on the time you will invest in the activity. Establish boundaries to keep your priorities front and center.

Limited Mission

People exchanging goods for services seek a business transaction. While unrelated income can provide "mission moments," such as the hospice group-room rental example, most customers will want you to solve their challenges as soon as possible. Be realistic about the amount of mission possible when you earn unrelated income.

Potential to Alienate or Eliminate Partners

If your nonprofit obtains corporate income, the mere suggestion that your nonprofit might earn income in one of the corporation's markets can extinguish your relationship forever. You are now a competitor. For instance, your nonprofit hospital decides to sell flowers in your gift shop. Your relationship with the florist across the street will not be the same after you announce this. To reduce this challenge, instead of going solo, create a partnership with the existing provider. Or enter markets only in places where the florist lacks interest. If all else fails, plan how you will replace the income you would otherwise have received from the florist.

Endowment Dream

Bessie Boley created an endowment of several million dollars for the organization she founded, Boley Centers. Over the years, the endowment has been an invaluable resource to the nonprofit that provides housing and services for individuals with special needs.

To win competitive government grants and expand, Boley Centers needs to own the land where new units will be built. When a desirable piece of property comes available, the foundation loans money to Boley Centers to buy it. Once funded, the loan is repaid with interest. Without site control, many expansion opportunities would be lost.

What if every nonprofit founder created a foundation and funded an endowment as part of a legacy? If you are a founder, create a foundation with your own resources or raise funds to create one to honor your work.

Missed Connections

The Berlin Wall divided the city of Berlin for decades. Here, "The Wall" symbolizes the dangers inherent in funding your nonprofit primarily with unrelated income. The danger is that the income becomes a barrier between you and those who care about your mission. The other six nonprofit income sources require the discipline of relationship with others around your mission. Unrelated income does not. For example, if you earn enough unrelated income, your board will not need to donate. This changes the board's behavior. Members become less engaged. Alleviate this challenge by developing new ways to retain your connections with the community and constituents.

Tax Fears

When I mention unrelated income in nonprofit workshops, a ripple of anxiety usually runs through the crowd. Leaders sometimes reject unrelated income because of tax concerns. Some fear their nonprofits will lose their tax-exempt status. With all due respect to taxing authorities, these fears are overblown. In one recent year, the IRS revoked the 501(c)(3) status of fewer than fifty organizations for unrelated business tax income concerns. Assuming similar future patterns, your odds of revocation are 1.5 million to 50, or 0.003 percent.

In some communities, nonprofits run into challenges with state and local taxing authorities. Yes, unrelated income does have tax consequences. Yes, it is possible that the IRS or Canada Revenue Agency or state or local authorities may challenge your status. For more background, listen to two US accountants about the topic on "Podcast #11" at kedconsult. com/podcasts. Then discuss your concerns with your accountant and, if warranted, your lawyer. Ask them to help you fulfill your obligations and reduce the risk of problems. Take note of any local, state, or province issues, and be proactive. Unrelated income, like all income, entails responsibility. Tax complications are a reason to be proactive—but not a reason to avoid unrelated income altogether.

To Recap

◆ Most nonprofits earn unrelated income in the form of interest on bank accounts, refunds, and snack-food receipts. Most could earn a lot more.

◆ Unrelated-income ideas can come from existing services, your customers, other nonprofits, and your own creativity.

◆ Even though unrelated income will never be your main focus, you can obtain it, overcome tax issues, and benefit from it.

Chapter Seven

Stream Seven—In-Kind Donations: When Cash Isn't King

IN THIS CHAPTER

···→ What is better than money?

···→ Obtain what you need most

···→ Why in-kind donations? Why not?

···→ Examples of success

The Oscar Mayer Wienermobile comes to town. Between scheduled events, it helps Seniors First deliver meals to homebound seniors. No money changes hands. Yet the seniors enjoy the entertainment, and both Oscar Mayer and Seniors First receive great press attention. The Wienermobile's visit represents another method nonprofits use to gather resources that fulfill their missions: in-kind donations.

In-kind gifts or in-kind donations are contributions of goods and services that nonprofits receive free or at low cost. This chapter focuses on in-kind gifts as a tool you can use to obtain needed resources. In-kind gifts include volunteer services, deep discounts, bartering, and other methods nonprofits use to acquire goods and services at below-market value. Potential sources include individuals, governments, corporations, foundations, and other nonprofits.

For the sector as a whole, in-kind gifts are difficult to measure. Top US corporations estimate that yearly in-kind giving exceeds $6 billion. Every year, volunteers give about $170 billion worth of time. These estimates fail to count the cans of tuna that Jim drops in food barrels, the cupcakes Anna makes for the PTA bake sale, and the blankets for the homeless that the Joneses donate where they worship.

How Can You Obtain In-Kind Gifts That Provide High Value?

"We need food for our darling kittens," a lighted sign on a busy highway announces. Like this animal shelter, you probably already ask for in-kind donations. To obtain them, you might use a lighted sign or an online wish list. You might request items from individuals. Or your supporters might identify your needs and provide them, such as the regular volunteer who sees your garden is running short of potting soil then brings a van load.

Many people are willing to help if you ask or when they become aware of your needs.

Like the ways suggested above, obtaining in-kind donations can be easy. Getting maximum benefit from them requires more effort. You need donations that provide essential items and services that help you do your mission. You want items and services that you would otherwise have to purchase. You want items that you can use immediately, not those you have to store for a year. You want items that help you reach the next level in your work—those that make a difference. You need in-kind donations for which you can authentically and enthusiastically thank the donor.

In-Kind Gifts 101

In-kind gifts or in-kind donations are gifts of goods or services, including volunteer time. The in-kind stream includes all noncash donations that nonprofits receive because they are nonprofits. Few statistics are available to calculate the value of these gifts. The in-kind source is extremely important to nonprofits.

principle

You can create strategies to receive in-kind gifts that help your nonprofit. One easy approach is finding ways to get items you regularly buy so that you can save your precious operating funds for other needs. Clothes to Kids in Florida provides children with school clothing. Even though it receives lots of donated clothing, it regularly runs short of socks and underwear. To encourage donating more of these items as in-kind gifts, the organization asks people to bring three-packs of socks to all meetings, gatherings, and events. When staff speaks at local clubs, they ask that attendees bring packs of kids' underwear.

If you need labor, not goods, design your operations to support volunteers doing the work either at your site or in their homes or offices. Provide first-class volunteer opportunities so people have fun while they work. This is not about providing refreshments. It is about making the task fun, interactive, and a chance to offer a real contribution. I recently was asked to provide pro bono consulting to a program that both my children had enjoyed. I agreed to do it on the condition that my college-aged child could come along and provide his ideas. This was a win for the program. My son offered a valid former-user perspective. It was a win for me since we would have a chance to work together to improve something we cared about.

Here is a six-step action plan to help your nonprofit gain maximum benefit from the in-kind goods and services you seek:

1. First, answer this question: From a big-picture perspective, what stops you from accomplishing more of your mission? If it's money, what specifically would you buy? If it's staff, what exactly would they do? What items specifically do you need? How might you receive these items or services as in-kind gifts? Jot some notes.

2. Inventory what you currently receive as in-kind donations. Tally both goods and volunteering, including committee and board member time. Review this information, and determine if you can obtain more of these items by making fresh efforts.

3. For items you do not currently receive, gather ideas about how you might obtain them. Who has what you need? Why would they want to give it to you? What benefits can you provide besides a thank-you or receipt? If you are not currently receiving it, what sources exist that might provide it to you? Go beyond the obvious. For instance, if you need electricity, your first thought will be the power company. Unfortunately, an in-kind donation here is unlikely since every nonprofit would soon clamor for equal treatment. Instead, ask an electrician to help you install energy-saving lights, and ask a local lighting store to donate the fixtures to reduce your bill long term. These approaches, especially if you have existing relationships, are much more likely to succeed.

4. Focus on obtaining a few, or even just one, item or service at a time. Avoid overwhelming the

> **Buy One, Give One**
>
> In One for One, a program of TOMS shoes and eyewear (and recently added coffee), the firm donates a pair of shoes to a child in need for every pair purchased. Through this program, TOMS has given over a million pairs of new shoes to children around the world.

stories from the real world

world with your needs. If you have a wish list, keep it short. Remember the sign asking for kitten food? It didn't ask for puppy, bird, and turtle food too.

5. Be specific. To make in-kind gifts most useful, be precise in your requests. For instance, a retreat center requested white twin-size cotton flat sheets after its generic requests for sheets yielded unusable full-, queen-, and king-size sheets.

6. Communicate the *why* behind your request. At a community event, a Goodwill director told the Goodwill story. Then he asked for donations and shared how the donations would be turned into jobs, services, and a better community. Be intentional about getting your in-kind messages out. Don't forget to remind people how their gifts help.

Why Do Individuals, Businesses, and Other Groups Donate?

Many of the reasons people give in-kind gifts are the same reasons they donate cash. In-kind gifts also offer some unique benefits.

They Are Tangible

People like to give gifts that do what they intend them to do, which is help people. In-kind giving is a concrete way to help. When I give my time, I can

---

Helping Children, Helping Teachers

A Gift for Teaching began in 1998 when founder Gary Landwirth looked for a way to recycle unwanted and surplus business supplies. Since then, the nonprofit has become a tri-county operation distributing more than $40,000 worth of free school supplies and incentives *daily*.

At its Free Stores, the nonprofit provides school supplies to the community's highest-need schools and classrooms. It offers tools to students who otherwise would have none. It makes sure teachers do not spend their own money for supplies. Thousands of companies, individuals, and volunteers donate items.

 **stories from the real world**

directly see its benefit. When I donate food, I can imagine the sound of the can opener cutting the metal lid edge before a local family eats dinner.

Offers a Way to Test

In-kind donations provide an opportunity for donors to sample a relationship with a given nonprofit. When I donate small goods to your organization, I gain an opportunity to learn more about you. When I volunteer, I gain an insider's view about your culture and operations. In short, in-kind giving provides a low-cost way for me to test a potential relationship with your nonprofit.

Solves Donor Challenges

We live in an era of cheap goods. Nonprofits that accept used goods help donors deal with clutter. In-kind giving often offers an emotionally satisfying experience. People like to buy toys for children at the holidays. Parents like knowing that their children's outgrown baby clothes will help someone in need.

Prevents Waste

Without the opportunities for donation that many nonprofits provide, more useful goods would go to landfills. Many for-profits actively donate to avoid tipping fees at waste-management sites. Likewise, lots of wonderful volunteer hours would be lost without a nonprofit offering a worthwhile experience.

It's Affordable

People often believe they aren't philanthropists if they can't make megadollar donations. Yet they still want to help. Giving an in-kind gift provides that opportunity.

What Are the Benefits of In-Kind Donations?

Nonprofits benefit from the in-kind gifts in at least four ways.

Low Cost or Free

Jeannie is everyone's favorite volunteer receptionist. Three days per week, she greets visitors. Jeannie's regular volunteering allows the nonprofit to hire one less staff member. Jeannie loves the opportunity to make a difference. The nonprofit loves her, and also the fact that her volunteering is an in-kind donation. For nonprofits, obtaining items or services free or heavily discounted is the key benefit of in-kind donations.

Tap Inaccessible Resources

Another benefit of in-kind gifts is the ability to tap into otherwise-inaccessible resources. Kate Spade, a well-known designer, agreed to be a special guest at an event that benefited the Ave Maria Preparatory School. She was willing to give her time, even though the school was new and relatively small, because one of her relatives attended the school. Besides people, nonprofits can sometimes access equipment, specialty items, and unique venues, such as the school group that held the prom at the White House when then-President Gerald Ford's daughter Susan was a teen.

Start Relationships

In-kind giving offers the opportunity to begin relationships with new people. The nonprofit can take advantage of the interactions surrounding

---

Can You Create Fan Days?

Instead of the usual items, Jonathan Toews, a professional ice hockey player with NHL's Chicago Blackhawks, developed fan-day experiences as an auction item. While each day would depend on the team's schedule, fan days might begin with four friends watching a practice from the bench. Before lunch, each of the friends might receive a team jersey with autographs. After lunch, they might take a behind-the-scenes stadium tour. The day could conclude with watching a game from a corporate box. Each fan experience generates around $5,000 to support the nonprofit that publishes *La Liberté*, Manitoba's only French-language provincial weekly newspaper.

A fan experience is also an outstanding example of a creative corporate in-kind gift. It provides substantial value to the person bidding and is low cost for the corporation. You can develop similar experiences with sports themes, but don't stop there. Consider visits to movie sets, VIP lunches, real estate tours, and other unique-to-your-community experiences.

stories from the real world

such a donation as the opportunity to start a conversation about your own nonprofit.

Large Potential

Your grocery store offers you a buy-one-get-one-free opportunity. You donate the free items to the food bank. So most in-kind gifts are small, right? While many are, many are not. Consider programs to collect donations of cars, boats, and vehicles. Also, consider Feeding America's store donation program, which collects food from grocery retailers. In one recent year, this effort gleaned 625 million pounds of food for the hungry. In-kind potential is as large as you decide to make it.

Challenges

Each nonprofit-income source involves advantages and challenges. With in-kind donations, you will want to take care that the lure of free or inexpensive does not blind you to its challenges. Here are several key in-kind challenges to anticipate, plus some suggestions on how to reduce your in-kind risk. Use these tips so your wish list does not become a regret list.

Not Free

Sometimes busy nonprofits overlook the fact no volunteer or good received is ever completely free. All in-kind donations require at least some time investment. Minutes must be invested to identify jobs, recruit, train, support volunteers, and recognize their gift. Donated items must be acknowledged, sorted, and distributed to where they will be used. To overcome this, invest and develop in-take and follow-up processes.

Wrong Stuff, Skills, Timing, Place . . .

Hurrah! Someone donated gravel for your back parking lot. Bummer. It's halfway across the country. Unlike cash or cash equivalents, an in-kind gift is by nature not easily transferable. To be useful, you need your in-kind gifts to be the right items or skills, at the right time, in the right place. If you accept the wrong "gift," you can destroy your nonprofit. More than one entity has closed after accepting real estate gifts that turned out to be toxic-waste sites.

To avoid the "wrong stuff" challenge, every nonprofit's board needs to develop, adopt, and use a gift-acceptance policy. You can find many examples online. To avoid toxic-waste sites, such policies usually require environmental reviews before property ownership is transferred. Your policy should also identify donors, such as corporations from whom it will not accept gifts because of potential harm to the nonprofit's reputation. Developing a policy now will help your board avoid disputes when a donor stands in the door offering a very attractive resource you know you should turn down.

Confusion

Another challenge with in-kind gifts is that they can cause confusion. In the first of two kinds of confusion, a person donates an in-kind gift and then is reluctant to give cash because "I already gave." The donors who deposit canned salmon into the donation barrel decide they have done their part to solve local hunger. Nonprofits can reduce this confusion by using in-kind opportunities to educate about mission-related needs.

Hurting the Ones You Love

This final challenge with in-kind gifts also involves donors. This is the second type of confusion. Donors seek to give useful gifts. Unfortunately, just like some of the holiday presents you receive, donors don't always understand your needs. Imagine that you are working with a Habitat for Humanity affiliate. A long-time donor just emailed you. The donor's deceased mother had a perfectly good house that the donor wants to provide for one the families on your waiting list. Unfortunately, the house's value is more than five times the selling price of Habitat homes. You want to sell the property and use the proceeds to build several houses and serve several families. To do so you, must thank the donor, educate the donor, share the new plan, convince the donor of the wisdom of this plan, and hope that you do not damage the relationship—whatever the outcome. In-kind gifts, despite everyone's best intentions, can be inappropriate and do require careful handling.

Up to this point, you learned about the different funding sources available. With your new understanding of the sources available to build your financial future, you are now ready to develop an income strategy for your nonprofit. Using the knowledge you have gained about these sources, manipulate and combine them to create your own unique income strategy and plan.

To Recap

◆ Most nonprofits obtain in-kind gifts and services.

◆ To provide your nonprofit the most help from in-kind resources and services, take an active approach to obtain them.

◆ The benefits of in-kind gifts are huge. They can build a community of support and provide you with much-needed items.

◆ The challenges of in-kind donations include donor confusion and receiving unwanted items.

Part Two

Sustainable Income at Your Nonprofit

The seven nonprofit-income streams discussed so far illustrate how the nonprofit sector as a whole obtains revenue. You, however, want to know how your nonprofit can obtain *more* income. Using the seven income streams, which can be adapted in endless ways, your leadership should decide on the best strategy for your nonprofit. This part of the book helps you explore others' successes and build a strategy and income plan.

Chapter Eight

Don't Develop Your Income Strategy Alone

IN THIS CHAPTER

···➔ Mining gold: what others know

···➔ Plagiarize from the best

···➔ Learn more: the 990, website, and interviews

···➔ Why copycats fail

···➔ Examples of success

When Michael Pastreich joined The Florida Orchestra as its president and CEO, the orchestra faced a structural deficit of $2.7 million, owed $2.5 million to financial institutions, and had a pile of unpaid bills. Worse, season subscriptions, which had been in decline for over a decade, plummeted by an additional 10 percent from the previous year. What Pastreich didn't know was that in the months ahead, he and the orchestra would face the worst recession since the Great Depression. Nonetheless, five years later, The Florida Orchestra became one of the most vibrant orchestras in the nation. The structural deficit soon dropped to less than $500,000. Seventeen concerts sold out in a recent year, while the subscriber base grew by an astounding 29 percent.

To what does Pastreich credit this amazing comeback? In part, discipline. "Success," he explains, "came from a plethora of small, incremental steps." Also, The Florida Orchestra found creative ways to fill the halls, eliminate

Strategy

A course of actions to reach a goal. The concept originated with the military. Generals plan how to win battles to win wars. A nonprofit-income strategy is the actions you take to earn or receive the donated income that achieves your goals. Like a logic model that you may have developed for your program outcomes, this is an economic logic model to fund your nonprofit.

 **finition**

the deficit, gain a clear artistic vision, and create internal alignment around these issues.

You, like The Florida Orchestra, can succeed despite the hurdles you face. By setting a limited number of specific goals and pursuing them, you can achieve income and mission success. The Florida Orchestra story is just one example of many, many nonprofit success stories.

Many who have succeeded will share their successes, and you can learn from their experiences. They can help you correct your assumptions, fine-tune efforts, and ease your journey. This chapter shares how.

One goal of your income strategy is that it uniquely fits your nonprofit skills and gifts. Designing an income strategy starts by gathering information about how others in the field, like you, solve their income challenge. Once you understand the solutions that work for others, you are in an even stronger position to consider your options.

Power Purchases

Second Harvest Food Bank of Central Florida developed a new mission-income stream that yields $500,000 per year. Realizing that many of its five hundred vendors (nonprofits that feed people) buy their food and food-related items (such as napkins) at big-box stores, the food bank developed Power Purchase. The Power Purchasing Center buys items in bulk and passes some of the savings to the vendors. With Power Purchase, the food bank receives new income and the vendors receive needed items for less than they previously paid.

 **stories from the real world**

You may already know components of your income strategy. For instance, Dr. Kent Lydecker, with the Museum of Fine Arts, shared in an interview: "You can't fund a museum solely on admissions. No one has yet made it on that model." Therefore, if your nonprofit is a museum, your income strategy must include not only admissions but other sources, as well. You might be aware of how organizations that are geographically close to you are funded. To create the best strategy, reach out to others. Study successful organizations in your field across the continent. Start with success stories for inspiration. (You might have found some ideas in these pages.) Then dig for pertinent details on the Internet. Later, seek personal interviews.

Gold Mining: What Others Know

Before 1953, people doubted if the top of Mount Everest could be reached. Edmund Hillary proved it could be done. Now a hundred people climb to the summit yearly. Before 1954, people doubted that anyone could run a mile in four minutes. In 1954, Roger Bannister astounded the world by running a mile in less than four minutes for the first time by any human. Now middle-distance runners frequently accomplish the feat. When you develop your nonprofit's income strategies, you need to answer two questions:

1. *Can it be done?*

2. *Can we do it?*

The answer to the first question is akin to learning that the four-minute mile barrier was broken and the summit of Mount Everest was reached. Once you know that it is possible, you need the answer to the second question. To learn if you can do it, find out more about experiences of those who have succeeded at the task in your field. The next section helps you identify these successes.

Finding the Best to Borrow from

To develop sustainable income, learn from nonprofits that successfully conquered the income challenge. Just any nonprofits in your field won't do. Find excellent ones.

How to Find Nonprofits Succeeding in Your Field

The following outlines an information-gathering process for learning from successes in your field. (Here we apply the process to income models. You can also use it for other new endeavors.)

❑ Identify seven to ten successful nonprofits in your field.

❑ Study those nonprofits' websites and public records to identify funding streams.

❑ Look for patterns. Is everyone, for instance, gung ho on corporate support?

❑ For any nonprofit you'd like to know more about, prepare a list of questions.

❑ Interview up to seven leaders by telephone or in person.

❑ Within twenty-four hours of your conversation, send a thank-you note. Jot down the lessons learned.

❑ Compare and contrast the information. Report what you learned to your decision makers.

❑ Decide which lessons to adopt.

to-do lists

Where can you find excellent examples of success in your field? Try the following:

- ◆ Well-known and mentioned examples

- ◆ Intriguing workshop leaders

- ◆ Nonprofits cited in publications

- ◆ Award recipients

- ◆ Referrals from associations where you are a member

Generate a generous list of nonprofits to study. Resist the temptation to focus only on those in your vicinity and those you know. Reaching new contacts will provide you with fresh ideas.

Who to Study: A Checklist

Learn Everything

To learn more about income in his field, Cliff Olstrom, executive director of Tampa Lighthouse for the Blind, created a database of over 250 nonprofit agencies that serve the blind. For each, he listed income and expenses, and he organized the data so he could compare the revenue streams of similar organizations, such as comparing guide-dog schools with other schools. This data allowed Lighthouse to review the fiscal experiences of other entities and to learn how Lighthouse compared with them.

While you might review hundreds of agencies, most nonprofits only need to focus on a small subset of similar nonprofits. Comparative information helps you create reasonable expectations and identify people to interview.

stories from the real world

Once you generate a list of nonprofits of interest, choose a half dozen or so to study in depth. Here is a checklist to help you narrow down your choices.

- ❑ Five-star operations. If you lead a four-star hotel and seek to excel, you study five-star hotels. In this case, pick out nonprofits with solid income strategies that are one solid step ahead of you.

- ❑ Distance makes the heart grow fonder. As you look for nonprofits to study, give preference to those at a distance. Why? Your success will not threaten their efforts. Your service areas and donors don't overlap. Besides, your success will give them a new partner and bragging rights. More importantly, the distance will provide you with more information and a better perspective. You probably already know something about others in your region. Go farther to gain richer information.

❑ In your list of nonprofits to study more, focus on those that recently succeeded. Entities that moved from being government funded twenty years ago can offer helpful advice. You will receive superior advice from entities that made the change successfully in the last three to five years. Conditions change rapidly. Seek nonprofits with recent successes.

❑ Travel in a similar vehicle. An excellent nonprofit with potential to study is one that created the income you seek under similar circumstances. For instance, if you want to develop more individual donations among your staff, look for a nonprofit known for this in a similar service area. Community size and culture matter. Funding a nonprofit in a resort community can be vastly different from funding it in a major metropolitan or rural area. Study from distant locations recently successful similar nonprofits.

Better Than Copying

When the Manasota Industry Council created a school-to-work program, it studied successful programs across the county with a focus on funding streams. These programs help high school students who are not college bound to create a career path during high school. Six leaders from seven programs were interviewed. The award-winning Louisville Education and Employment Partnership (LEEP) became the council's key model. LEEP was located in a metropolitan area of similar size, the program was nationally recognized, and staff was generous with information. With the knowledge they gathered from LEEP and six other programs, the council developed a school-to-work program, won $100,000 in local startup funding and, later, $1 million in federal funding.

stories from the real world

Getting Information: Federal Reports, Websites, Interviews, and More

Once you identify nonprofits with attractive income streams to study, how can you learn more? This section reviews two common information sources.

Using your computer, smartphone, or tablet, look at the following:

◆ *The nonprofit's website.* Look for annual reports, press releases, and program data. A drawback here is that this information will not always tell you about success, just that it dabbles in the area.

◆ *The results of a search.* You can often find interesting articles about the nonprofit with a general Internet search. Who else is talking about them?

◆ *Nonprofit databases.* In the United States, much financial information can be gained through nonprofit databases. As of this writing, two important sites are Charity Navigator and GuideStar. In Canada, less public information is available. You can often obtain lists of nonprofits in different regions from the Canada Revenue Agency website. Also, search the Industry Canada website.

◆ *How to request information.* You can often obtain pertinent documents with an email request.

All That Glitters Is Not Nonprofit Gold

During an interview, a nonprofit consultant who specializes in providing interim executive director services learned that her potential customer was actually two nonprofits, each with its own set of books. The nonprofit that was doing well was the one shared publicly. The other was the real story. Ouch! In your hunt for experts, be sure that what shines is gold.

practical tip

The Best Source: Conversations

When you seek to learn about processes that create success, nothing substitutes for a one-on-one conversation with a staff member who is an expert on the income you seek. In this setting, you can often engage the interviewee in doing some analysis of why things work.

While everyone in the sector is universally busy, most people consider it a compliment when asked about their success. The people you contact may even be hoping that someone will notice and ask for their wisdom. If you are unsure how to proceed, send an email or letter to introduce yourself. Share a time that you will call, and then set an interview time. Before you ask for an interview, however, do your homework. Study all the information publicly available. Prepare your questions.

What You Can Learn

Every study will be unique, but here is a brief list of the value you can obtain by studying successful nonprofits:

◆ What works and why

◆ Fresh ideas

◆ Practical hints, tips, and guidelines

◆ Helpful resources

◆ Easy and hard "spots" in the income development process

◆ Insights into the problems and opportunities

◆ A contact, and perhaps a friend, for future questions

Gaining peace of mind is not on the list—but is also likely. Someone who is successful at what you want to do can affirm that your goal is not only possible but realistic. To succeed, learn from nonprofit leaders who have "been there, done that."

Don't Be a Copycat

"Welcome to the restaurant. I'm Joe. I'll be your server tonight." The first restaurant that used this greeting must have been wildly successful. Now

Sample Interview Questions

For the interview, create a form with the questions organized logically, with space for answers. Use it as a flexible tool to make sure you cover what you need to know, even if an interviewee rambles. By asking similar questions in each interview, you can compare organizations and identify trends.

The following questions would work for an interview about all seven income streams:

☐ Where does your current funding come from? Help me understand your income history. How did the organization arrive at this juncture?

☐ What is the most challenging income source for you to earn? How have you overcome the challenge?

☐ What is the most interesting way your nonprofit raises money?

☐ What has surprised you about obtaining income?

☐ What are your earned sources? How big is your customer base? Is it shrinking, growing, stable? Why?

☐ Tell me about your donations. How large is your donor base? Your development staff? Can you share a typical donor experience?

☐ In terms of raising income, what are the characteristics of your community and your local economic trends?

☐ How would you prefer to be funded? What funding streams do you plan to grow in the future?

☐ If you were starting over, what would you do differently? Why?

☐ Given my goals, what other organizations should I interview?

it's so ubiquitous you can use it to portend a mediocre meal. Compare this with the server who, sensing you are very hungry, volunteers to help you pick an appetizer you can be eating in five minutes. The first greeting is a great example of why copying fails. The second is an example of what the first sought to accomplish—a pleasant meal that creates repeat customers. Copying results in overt behavioral changes. Adapting another's successful results changes beliefs, attitudes, and processes.

As you study others, seek to understand the processes they used to create the overt behavior changes. Never just copy. In the short run, copying will seem quicker—until it fails to work. To gain understanding of the whole success process, talk to several people doing what you wish to emulate.

Of course, once you understand the process, you still need to adapt it to your setting and fine-tune it over time. What does this fine-tuning look like? You go to a workshop and learn to send thank-you notes for donations within forty-eight hours. The notes you write focus on your organization. When you receive a note from another nonprofit for a donation you made, you learn something important. The other nonprofit's note is all about you. It states how helpful you have been and how your gift will be used. In response, you fine-tune your thank-you notes to focus

---

Copying Versus Adapting

Copying. You receive a copy of an annual letter that was successful at a similar nonprofit. You update it and add one of your stories. You send it out one year later, cross your fingers, and hope that you will reap the same outcome. You don't.

Adapting. You receive the same letter. You contact staff at the nonprofit who wrote it. You learn the "why" behind the content and about the mailing lists used, etc. In short, you gain a full understanding of the process used before, during, and after mailing the letter. You learn about all the related activities, such as press releases, blogs, and Twitter posts. With this knowledge, you establish a plan for your annual appeal. After you send it, you don't just cross your fingers. You're engaged in supportive activities. In a month, you realize that your success will surpass that of the nonprofit that taught you. Build on the success of others.

Example

on the donor. Fine-tuning involves making continual improvements that provide better and better results.

Adapting successful ideas strengthens your work. Combine what you now do with what you learn from others to create superior results. Look beyond the successful actions. Dig deeper. Learn the process and thinking that make those outward actions the right behavior for each situation. Success comes from using the right processes and disciplined fine-tuning. This is the discipline that The Florida Orchestra used to succeed: the plethora of small, incremental steps.

To Recap

♦ To develop an income strategy using the seven nonprofit income streams, study the successes of others in your field.

♦ Be selective when you choose nonprofits to study.

♦ Collect information. Use the Internet. Review public documents. Conduct personal interviews.

♦ Never copy others. Instead, adjust what you learn about another organization's successes to your setting. Use the other nonprofit's successes as your starting point.

Chapter Nine

Money, Resources, and Beyond

IN THIS CHAPTER

····→ Create your strategy and income plan

····→ Find income sweet spots

····→ Work with your new opportunities

····→ Sustainable income for your nonprofit

A t Junior Achievement affiliates, the traditional funding strategy relies on corporate income. Businesses are interested in the mission to help young people understand the economics of life. Yet many regions lack Fortune 500 corporations. Can a Junior Achievement affiliate survive when large corporations are scarce? Yes, Junior Achievement of Tampa Bay, Inc., provides a model.

A third of this affiliate's income comes from sporting events involving golf, bowling, and running. While almost no expert recommends building a nonprofit-income strategy around special events, this strategy works here. In another deviation from traditional Junior Achievement income strategy, the affiliate partners with a workforce development board to earn $800,000 yearly in government funds. It also receives corporate funding. Besides donations, they obtain sponsorships for a virtual JA BizTown, a minicity where students experience the working world. Here leading community businesses buy storefront names in a virtual town used by school students. Together, these funding streams create a successful income strategy for

Junior Achievement of Tampa Bay. How successful? Its income has grown in each of the past twenty-four years.

Find Sweet Spots

In the previous chapter, you learned to study successful nonprofits in your field. This chapter discusses other strategy considerations and income planning. To be sustainable, each nonprofit must find a unique combination of income sources and weave them together into a strategy for the organization. The seven income streams—mission, individual donations, governments, foundations, corporations, unrelated income, and in-kind gifts—represent the choices you can use in your strategy. To develop an income strategy for your nonprofit, use the models you found in the field plus the following six ideas:

1. Fit

Every nonprofit has a different history, skills, and community. Not all income sources fit each nonprofit the same. The income sources and strategy you select need to fit your nonprofit.

2. Major in the Majors

Build a strategy that includes at least one, if not all, the top-three nonprofit-income sources—that is, mission revenue, individual donations, and/or government funding. Success is possible if you choose not to focus on receiving income from these streams. However, it will be more difficult. Together, these three streams constitute over 75 percent of nonprofit income. Include one or more of the big income streams in your strategy.

3. Less Is More

Most nonprofits start with one or two funding streams and, as opportunities arise over time, dabble in them all. Successful nonprofits take it one step farther. They focus on the one, two, or maybe three interactive streams. The resulting strategy fits them, the marketplace, and the leaders' skills. For instance, Goodwill Industries of Central Florida focuses on obtaining in-kind used goods *and* mission income.

4. Unique

As you develop an income strategy, focus on sources that fit you, your market, and your leaders' skills. Sarasota Goodwill's strategy focuses on obtaining in-kind and mission income, like Central Florida Goodwill. Unlike Central Florida Goodwill, it adds individual donations to the mix. These two different strategies of two sister agencies reflect the nature of their communities and the bent and beliefs of current and past leadership. Develop an income strategy informed by others but unique to your nonprofit.

5. Dual Purpose

In a well-designed income portfolio, each funding stream serves a purpose that provides income plus other benefits. These benefits tie logically into your mission and strengthen your culture. For instance, you seek individual donations because these provide income. They also create a pool of people who will support legislative changes to make your mission unnecessary in time.

Turning In-Kind Gifts into Cash

Goodwill takes gently used goods from generous donors and turns them into money to help people. This strategy deftly combines in-kind donations and mission income to create sustainable income. According to Bill Oakley, the president/CEO of Goodwill Industries of Central Florida, Inc., reliance on in-kind donations/gifts works because "everyone owns items that are no longer useful. Most of us would like someone to get value from them." When it accepts used items and promises to make good use of them, Goodwill satisfies some of your emotional needs.

In Central Florida, this concept has become a complex multi-million-dollar operation. Here, Goodwill's operations collect goods and operate used-clothing stores. The nonprofit also operates an online outlet for books, a computer-recycling center, markets for corrugated cardboard and metal, and a thrift store. Shoppers sort through clothing on large tables at the store, and merchandise is replaced every twenty-four hours. Any remaining goods are sold for rags.

 stories from the real world

---

6. Commit and Invest

Do your homework, select a strategy, and stick with it. Commitment is critical because success with any given income source will be a long-term endeavor built on numerous connected actions. Commitment provides the time and momentum staff and leaders need to master the different processes involved in obtaining each income stream. Without commitment, your supporters will go, "Oh pretty," when new income opportunities arise. When your budget is tight, commitment to the current path demands that you find a way to overcome them rather than abandon the strategy and chase after interesting but untested income ideas.

In any given nonprofit journey, nonprofit leaders face frequent anxiety about the nonprofit's current income. Many leaders focus only on short-term dollars. To create sustainable income, you need to avoid the vicious cycle of worrying about current income while doing nothing to create long-term income. Successful organizations grow beyond this scarcity mindset. They use the selected strategy as a framework and invest in tomorrow's income today. Without this improvement, tomorrow will bring you only a slightly different flavor of today's challenges. Establish a new pattern of commitment and investment. Your strategy is your best hope for income success. That is why you pick it.

Boards, staff, and volunteers all need to believe in the strategy. That's why I strongly recommend that you study the sources to find what fits, explore successful models, and then develop your own unique strategy. A strategy created in this manner gives you something solid to cling to through the storms ahead.

Income Strategy and Income Plans

The long-term goal of your strategy is to provide your nonprofit with plenty of income. This strategy provides a macro view of how you will achieve sustainable income. It focuses on the smartest approach for your situation. It's a bit like looking at a large map, identifying your destination, and then running your finger along the major highways from where you are to your destination.

In contrast, your income plan focuses on steps to move you toward the goal, using the approaches your strategy identifies. Using both the strategy and the plan moves you toward your goal. Both the strategy and the plan look to the future and work from it. Both are fine-tuned by reality. The strategy shows how to use the expressway. The plan looks ahead but focuses on the specifics. Do I go around Chicago or through it? The plan takes into account that the expressway is under construction and that the fastest route is a detour through the city.

Strategies cleverly develop income by building on your strengths, skills, and wisdom. With these as givens, what is the smartest way for you to get to your vision? One Goodwill Industries affiliate's strategy is to maximize

Strategy Map   Navigation Plan

the used goods it receives from customers. An income plan, in contrast, lays out how Goodwill will open numerous donation sites. Similarly, Mote Marine Laboratories' strategy is to help individual donors fund its research, since government funding is insufficient. Its plans led to opening live animal exhibits to engage the community and grow more donors. The Florida Center for Early Childhood, highlighted in the sidebar, changed its strategy to obtain more individual donors. Its plan called for getting board members more active.

After you develop an income strategy, plan how you will use it now to move toward your goal. Useful income plans cover the next quarter, six months, or year. The following guidelines will help you plan. They complement other common planning guidelines, such as identifying measureable steps and assigning responsibilities.

Build from Current Sources

If your strategy calls for new sources, continue to earn your existing income as much as possible while you make the transition. For instance, if your strategy is to obtain more individual donations instead of government income, continue to obtain the government funds while you develop an individual donor base. You might, for example, find new donors to fund people who need your service but don't qualify for it under government rules.

Master Your Sources

Plan to become an expert in your key income sources. In *The Tipping Point*, Malcolm Gladwell teaches that expertise takes ten thousand hours. Nonprofits that solve the income challenges invest this amount of time and more in mastering the key income sources. Obtaining sustainable income is not done-in-a-day stuff. Learn and practice. Read, attend events, and convey to those around you what you learned. In your plan, don't set out to learn everything. Instead, focus on the income streams most important to your nonprofit. Plan to be masters.

Link Effort to Efforts

As you plan, organize your activities so that they connect to other opportunities. For instance, make your gala part of a series of events to develop relationships with more individual donors. Instead of ending at midnight, end your gala sixty days later—after you have contacted every attendee and invited each to tour your

---

The Rewards of Planning Ahead

Even without a crystal ball, staff at The Florida Center for Early Childhood foresaw significant state funding cuts in the future. Combining this foresight with disciplined actions, staff forged a new income strategy that included pursuing existing sources and growing individual donations. The hardest part of executing the plan, according to Linda Greaves, vice president of leadership and development, was finding ways to get board members comfortable with their new roles. Over several years, the center recruited new members who understood the necessity for the new income stream and actively supported it. When the predicted funding cuts arrived, the center had new donors and income in place.

 **stories from the real world**

site. Then, as each site visit concludes, invite these visitors to a special tea in ninety days. At the tea, invite people to a special lecture, and so forth. You can also do this on the individual level and weave in donor and non-donor events. If you have lunch with a potential donor, plan and introduce the idea about your next interaction at the end of lunch. Link events and interactions so that they build on each other. This avoids starting and stopping, creates expectations, helps you think sequentially, and saves marketing efforts and resources.

Be Opportunistic

Good income planning anticipates opportunities. Plan to continue seeking easy income, no matter its source. Even if your strategy calls for you to avoid grants, plan to continue requesting the one from the foundation that provides $5,000 each year with a one-page letter. Additionally, besides easy opportunities, continue to pursue income that provides other benefits, even if the income is minimal or the "wrong kind." Some sources provide great contacts, new skills, and branding. Follow your strategy, but take calculated high-value detours.

Diversify Over Time

The more viable and diverse your nonprofit's funding streams, the greater your odds of recovering when conditions change. Over time, conditions and beliefs will change. While government funding has experienced the most recent change, other income streams are not immune to fluctuations. For instance, suppose you are highly focused on individual donors and a board scandal makes headlines for weeks in your community. Everyone will be very thankful that you can increase your other income streams until the furor abates.

Once you master your key income streams, focus efforts on mastering other streams to provide your nonprofit bounce-back potential. If existing sources are doing well, most nonprofits can add a new source every three to five years.

Working with New Income Opportunities

In reality, healthy nonprofit leadership can't pursue every income idea, due to time and resource limits. As new opportunities arrive, resist the temptation to spend huge amounts of time exploring new ideas until after you categorize them into one of the seven income streams where you can compare them with similar opportunities.

If it is not obvious which income stream an opportunity belongs to, determine if the money will be earned, donated, or both. This will help you narrow down the options. Donated income includes in-kind donations and cash from individuals, foundations, and other grant-giving entities—and ' sometimes corporations. Earned income includes mission, government, and unrelated income—and sometimes corporate funds.

If you are still stuck about how to categorize an opportunity, consider who will make the decision to provide the money or resource. If you are still unsure, assign the opportunity to a "best guess" income category you want to grow. You can often shape opportunities to fit your needs. For instance, you volunteer with a friends-of-a-park group. Someone suggests you hold a garage sale. You can place this opportunity in the unrelated income category. However, since your strategy calls for earning more mission income, you can elect to place it in mission income by shaping it. In this case, instead of just selling used goods, make it a sale of items for park use, such as canoes, picnic goods, hiking shoes, and guidebooks.

Sorting your opportunities reduces confusion. Comparison with similar options improves decision-making. For example, you categorize the suggestion of a special event as an individual-donations opportunity. Now you are in excellent position to decide if it should be added to your current efforts or if you have a more effective opportunity you can pursue instead.

If you find you have many opportunities to review, consider forming a task group to sort, study, and determine how quickly to pilot opportunities. The Museum of Science and Industry in Tampa, Florida, developed a team that periodically evaluates income opportunities.

Mission Accomplished: Nonprofit Income

In this book, you learned about the biggest three sources of nonprofit income: mission income, individual donations, and government funding. You learned about the other small but important players: foundations and other grant-giving entities, corporations, and unrelated income. You were reminded about the immense value of in-kind donations. You also discovered how to study excellent models of income success and, finally, received guidance about creating a long-term income strategy and short-term plans.

The seven income sources are tools to help you achieve your mission. Choose and use these income streams, as appropriate. Just as you learn to use the key features on your cell phone, learn to use the tools you need. While true expertise will come over time, success will come sooner. Often you don't need to be an unbelievable expert to obtain income. In the nonprofit world, good work and smart approaches succeed, even if the tool user is still learning.

Your mission is your trump card. People want you to succeed. They will help with your mission—if you ask. In the light of these principles, you will find it easier to build a bridge to your sustainable income. Nearly every nonprofit has significant, untapped opportunities to diversify and grow its sources of income. The field is in the midst of evolving to healthier, more sustainable funding. You can succeed.

To Recap

◆ Weave the seven nonprofit-income sources together to form an income strategy for your nonprofit.

◆ Your skills, experience, and mission point you to certain income streams. Build on them.

◆ Develop and commit to a unique income strategy for your nonprofit that fits your organization, focuses on a few key sources, and includes at least one from the three largest income streams.

◆ Once you develop your strategy, create a plan to obtain income. Start with your current resources. Be opportunistic and master your key income streams. Link as many efforts as possible into a stream of related events. Finally, over time, add new income streams.

◆ In these chapters, you studied the seven nonprofit-income streams from the point of view of those who provide the income to nonprofits. Remember this viewpoint as you fund your nonprofit.

Appendix A

Glossary

Bequest: This is an individual gift given to a nonprofit from a donor's estate or will.

Case: A case is the reason, often written, your nonprofit needs funds and how having them will change or improve lives. Strong cases include emotional and logical information about the need for and the benefits of your work.

Cause marketing: Cause marketing is a business technique. Here a business promotes both the nonprofit and its own products or services. For the privilege of doing so, the business pays the nonprofit a percentage of sales or a set dollar amount.

Challenge grant: A challenge grant is a funding commitment to your nonprofit that requires you to raise, by a deadline, a certain amount of dollars from other sources. Raise the additional funds, and the funder gives you the challenge grant.

CLAT (charitable lead annuity trust): A CLAT is a type of planned gift. It is distinguished by being an irrevocable trust funded by a donor. In this case, the trust pays a fixed amount of income to the nonprofit for a number of years or while the donor lives. When the term ends, any remaining assets are distributed to the donor or the donor's heirs.

Community foundation: The community foundation serves a specific group of people, such as the residents of Toronto, or a subpopulation, such as Lutherans. Community foundations collect funds from a variety of donors, earn management fees on the funds, and oversee grant awards to nonprofits based on the goals of the donors and foundation.

Corporate income: Corporate income is nonprofit income from a business, corporation, or for-profit entity.

CRAT (charitable remainder annuity trust): A CRAT is a type of planned gift. It is similar to a CRUT (see below), with the exception that the agreement provides the donor a *set* amount of yearly income. The amount is agreed upon when the trust is established.

CRUT (charitable remainder unitrust): A CRUT is a type of planned gift. It is a trust wherein a donor irrevocably transfers assets to a nonprofit, which becomes the trustee. The nonprofit then invests the assets and pays the donor annual income from the asset's earnings. The income varies. At the donor's death, any remaining assets belong to the nonprofit.

Culture of philanthropy: A culture of philanthropy is a set of shared operating values around the role of individual donations in a nonprofit. These values include that everyone has a role to play in obtaining and giving donations at the highest level possible. In a culture of philanthropy, the board, staff, volunteers, customers, and others involved in a nonprofit live out these values.

Earmark: Nonprofits obtain earmark funds by working with elected government officials. The officials insert funding appropriations into government budgets and other documents. If the legislation passes, the nonprofit receives the funding award after executing a contract with the government.

The gap: The gap is the shortfall between the easy, expected annual money and what you really need to operate each year.

The givens: In this book, "the givens" describe income your nonprofit counts on, year to year.

Government funding: Government funding is earned revenue obtained by offering services—usually for community good—paid for by the government. This funding usually requires extensive paperwork.

Grant: A grant is money given to a nonprofit to complete a specific activity or project.

Grant-giving entity: A grant-giving entity is a private foundation, community foundation, federated fund (such as United Way), or other group that distributes funds to nonprofits, generally in a competitive process involving a written request.

Income plan: The income plan is a written list of specific activities that, when completed, help you reach or move you toward your revenue goal. It is helpful to revisit the plan annually.

Income strategy: The income strategy is a course of actions to reach a goal. The concept originated with the military, where generals planned how to win battles to win wars. In terms of income, strategies involve high-level, big-picture ideas that take advantage of your skills and gifts, and work around your shortcomings.

Individual donations: Gifts from individuals and families are individual donations.

In-kind donations: In-kind donations are contributions of goods and services that nonprofits receive free or at low cost.

Major gift: A major gift is an individual donation on such magnitude that it excites everyone at your nonprofit. Every nonprofit determines its own definition of major gift, and the definition often changes over time.

Mission: Your mission is the human or societal situation your organization addresses.

Mission income: Mission income is funding your nonprofit earns by doing its mission and providing services or products associated with it.

Other income: Other income is revenue that your nonprofit earns from providing a service or from selling goods when the product or service has little or no relationship to your mission.

Overhead: Expenditures you make to cover the costs of operating your nonprofit are overhead. Traditionally, expenses related to delivering programs and/or doing your mission are excluded from a calculation of overhead.

Planned gift: Planned gifts are donations that require individual preplanning. Planned gifts often include assets such as shares of stock or a piece of property. The donor's personal advisor—such as a CPA, lawyer, and/or financial planner—often participates in the decision-making and execution process.

Private foundation: A private foundation is a legal entity that owns a large corpus of funds that earns interest in the market. By law, a percentage of the corpus must be given to qualified nonprofits. Those who fund private foundations are usually wealthy families and corporations.

Prospect research: Prospect research is the process of gathering public information about individual donors to learn their potential for making a major gift and that gift's potential size.

Public-nonprofit partnership: Government entities often provide funding to nonprofit organizations to solve complex community challenges. These public-nonprofit partnerships address such issues as homelessness, increasing voter registrations, and changing neighborhoods.

Sliding scale: Fees for services or products that are incrementally adjusted based on the customer's income and family size or other criteria are described as sliding scale.

Special event: A special event is an event designed to raise money, increase relationships with current donors, and ideally create new friends for the nonprofit.

Sponsorship: A sponsorship can simply involve a nonprofit receiving cash support from a business or other entity in exchange for recognition at a special event. The sponsorship also can be broader. Well-developed sponsorships involve packages that include advertising, cause marketing, events, a donation, and ways to experience the business's service or product.

Stewardship: In the nonprofit setting, stewardship is the act of caring for donors. This caring includes sharing your gratitude, expressing how the donor's gifts helped, how the gift(s) served those the donor intended to help, and telling how else the donor might engage in your nonprofit's work.

Appendix B

Resources

The Association of Fundraising Professionals (AFP): AFP is a "professional association of individuals and organizations that generate philanthropic support for a wide variety of charitable institutions." Chapters meet throughout North America to learn about fundraising topics. See afpnet.org.

BoardSource: BoardSource is a national organization "for funders, partners, and nonprofit leaders who want to magnify their impact within their community through exceptional governance practices." This is a useful resource for sample policies, such as the gift-acceptance policy. Some resources are free. Others require a nominal fee. See boardsource.org.

Canada Revenue Agency: The Canada Revenue Agency maintains a website where you can learn more about Canadian charities. Here you can view a charity's T3010 information return. See cra-arc.gc.ca/charities.

CharityChannel: This website, professional community, and nonprofit resource connects nonprofit colleagues around the corner and around the world. The site offers numerous practical resources for the nonprofit practitioner. See charitychannel.com.

Charity Navigator: As of this writing, Charity Navigator is the largest evaluator of charities in the United States. Some of your donors will review this site to learn more about your nonprofit before they give to you. The site offers information on its evaluation methodology that's used to help determine if your nonprofit meets or exceeds certain standards. See charitynavigator.org.

Community Foundation Locator: The Council on Foundations provides a map to help you identify community foundations that serve your area. See cof.org/community-foundation-locator.

Foundation Center: Foundation Center operates a useful website for learning about foundations in the United States and their funding patterns. When you learn the name of a foundation, use the Foundation Finder to review that funder's IRS records. While you can purchase access to the grants database, some of the databases are free at cooperating collections sites, which include some libraries, community foundations, and resource centers. See foundationcenter.org.

Grants.gov: The primary website for researching discretionary government grants is grants.gov. Here you can access a database of twenty-six federal grant-making agencies in the United States. See grants.gov.

GuideStar: Use GuideStar's website to learn about a specific nonprofit. See guidestar.org.

Karen Eber Davis Consulting: My website contains over one hundred free articles, podcasts, videos, and back issues of the column *Your Ingenious Nonprofit* and the newsletter *Added Value*. Updates to this book will be posted on this site as well. Visit kedconsult.com.

Lists of employers that provide matching grants: To find employers that provide grants that match employee donations, type these words into a web search: "employer matching grant." I found several lists of employers.

The Partnership for Philanthropic Planning: This group promotes research, best practices, education, and gift-planning standards. Over one hundred affiliated local organizations hold regular meetings where you can learn more about planned giving and meet professional advisors. Go to pppnet.org.

Philanthropy News Digest: This publication of the Foundation Center provides information and links to current request for proposals, or RFPs, which are short-term grant opportunities. See philanthropynewsdigest.org/rfps.

Index

If you enjoyed this book, you'll want to pick up the other books in the CharityChannel Press **In the Trenches**™ series.

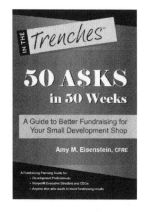

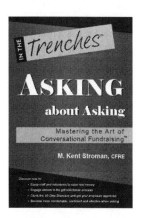

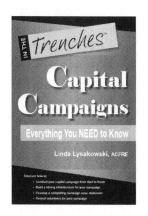

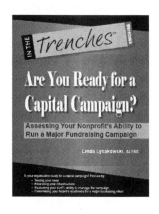

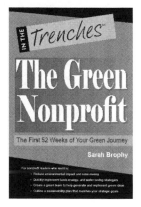

CharityChannel.com/bookstore

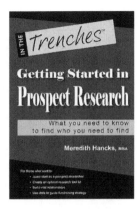

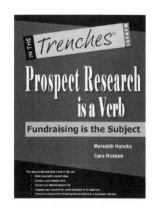

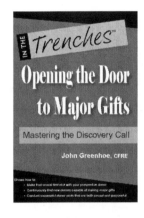

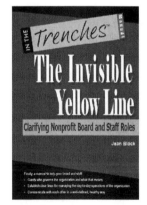

CharityChannel.com/bookstore

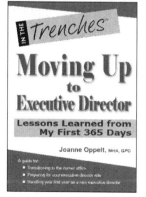

CharityChannel.com/bookstore

And now introducing **For the GENIUS® Press,** an imprint that produces books on just about any topic that people want to learn. You don't have to be a genius to read a **GENIUS** book, but you'll sure be smarter once you do!

ForTheGENIUS.com/bookstore

Made in the USA
San Bernardino, CA
06 September 2016